The Frog Who Croaked Blue

D0145466

As little Edgar Curtis lay on his porch, he remarked to his mother how the noise of the rifle range was black, the chirp of the cricket was red, and the croak of the frog was bluish. Edgar, like many other people, has synesthesia – a fascinating condition in which music can have color, words can have taste, and time and numbers float through space.

Everyone will be closely acquainted with at least six or seven people who have synesthesia but you may not yet know who they are because, until very recently, synesthesia was largely hidden and unknown. Now science is uncovering its secrets and the findings are leading to a radical rethink about how our senses are organized. In this timely and thought-provoking book, Jamie Ward argues that sensory mixing is the norm even though only a few of us cross the barrier into the realms of synesthesia.

How is it possible to experience color when no color is there? Why do some people experience touch when they see someone else being touched? Can blind people be made to see again by using their other senses? Why do scientists no longer believe that there are five senses? How does the food industry exploit the links that exist between our senses? Does synesthesia have a function? *The Frog Who Croaked Blue* explores all these questions in a lucid and entertaining way, making it fascinating reading for anyone with an interest in the intriguing workings of the mind.

 **Dr Jamie Ward** is a Senior Lecturer at the University of Sussex, UK, and is one of the world's leading experts on synesthesia. He has published over 40 scientific papers and several books. In addition, he has contributed to the public understanding of science through numerous talks and media coverage in newspapers, radio and television including documentaries produced by the Discovery Channel and BBC Horizon.

The Frog Who Croaked Blue

Synesthesia and the Mixing of the Senses

Jamie Ward

LONDON AND NEW YORK

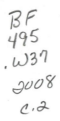
First published 2008
by Routledge
27 Church Road, Hove, East Sussex BN3 2FA

Simultaneously published in the USA and Canada
by Routledge
270 Madison Avenue, New York, NY 10016

Routledge is an imprint of the Taylor & Francis Group, an Informa business

© 2008 Jamie Ward

Typeset in New Century Schoolbook by Garfield Morgan,
Swansea, West Glamorgan
Printed and bound in Great Britain by TJ International Ltd
Padstow, Cornwall
Cover design by Hannah Armstrong

British Library Cataloguing in Publication Data
A catalogue record for this book is available from the British Library

Library of Congress Cataloging in Publication Data
Ward, Jamie.
    The frog who croaked blue : synesthesia and the mixing of the senses /
Jamie Ward.
        p. cm.
    Includes bibliographical references and index.
    ISBN 978-0-415-43013-5 (hardcover) – ISBN 978-0-415-43014-2 (pbk.)
1. Synesthesia. I. Title.
    BF495.W37 2008
    152.1'89–dc22

                                                                    2007051022

ISBN 978-0-415-43013-5 (hbk)
ISBN 978-0-415-43014-2 (pbk)

Dedication

For Spike and Stan

Contents

List of figures		ix
Preface		xi
The frog who croaked blue		xiii
1	**The colorful albino**	1
2	**Counting on the senses**	31
3	**An altered reality**	59
4	**The screen in my forehead**	89
5	**Beyond the senses**	117
	Notes	141
	References	155
	Index	169
	Further information on the web	175

List of figures

Figures

1 Debbie experiences numbers arranged in space   4
2 The two bars move together and then move apart:
   do they collide or pass in the middle?   47
3 A model of synesthesia   61
4 This ambiguous figure can be interpreted as
   either Es or an F   85
5 Synesthesia for the letter A is diminished in a
   hard task relative to an easy task   86
6 The rubber hand illusion   94
7 Claire experiences her days of the week as a
   continuous spatial landscape in front of her   107
8 Daniel Tammet visualizes the first 100 digits of
   pi as undulating colored spatial landscape   112
9 Which of these shapes should be called 'Bouba'
   and which 'Kiki'?   132

Preface

I first came across synesthesia in 2000. A friend of mine, Nick, happened to mention that his housemate had it. I had never heard of synesthesia even though, at this time, I already had a degree in natural sciences and a PhD in psychology, and was a lecturer in neuropsychology. Synesthesia was just not a topic that was commonly heard about back then. At the same time as I discovered synesthesia, and found someone who had it, there was coincidentally a visiting lecture in London given by V.S. Ramachandran. This triggered my enthusiasm and persuaded me that the topic is scientifically respectable (although others remain to be persuaded!). It was this combination of factors that drew me in to synesthesia research. I could never have believed that it would end up becoming my main area of research. Synesthesia has come a long way in terms of both what is known about it, and in terms of how many people have heard of it. This book represents the culmination of my knowledge over the past seven years. It is not the final word on synesthesia, but it represents a timely appraisal of where we are at.

The book is organized into five chapters. The first chapter covers the history of research into synesthesia, which is, surprisingly, not well known and is often inadvertently misrepresented by others who are active in the field. The chapter also considers, in very simple terms, how the brain can produce visual experiences when there is nothing out there to be seen – even in people who are blind. The second chapter deals with the 'mixing of the senses' part of the book's subtitle. It challenges the notion that our senses are strictly separable. The third chapter pulls together different strands of the previous chapters to outline a more general theory of synesthesia and how it relates to more typical forms of multisensory perception. The fourth chapter deals with how the brain creates a sense of space using various sorts of internal 'maps', and how space is important not only for perception but also for thinking and remembering. The final chapter considers the possible role of synesthesia beyond the senses. Does it have implications for creativity, language or memory?

The ideas in this book have been shaped through collaborative discussions with others. A significant part of the research was done with Julia Simner in Edinburgh. I worked closely with a number of colleagues in London over several years, who deserve particular mention; these include Noam Sagiv, James Collins and Michael Banissy. Many other researchers worldwide have been influential in shaping my ideas and are too numerous to list. I give due credit and thanks in the accompanying notes and references.

At Routledge (and Psychology Press), I'd like to thank Mike Forster for giving me the initial confidence and encouragement to write this book and Becci Waldron, who helped to pull it together and market the final product. Adrian, from Raft, provided excellent advice on promotion of the book. If you are reading this book now, then perhaps it worked.

Jamie Ward
Brighton, November 2007

The Frog Who Croaked Blue

Edgar Curtis is the son of Professor and Mrs. O.F. Curtis of Cornell University. At the time of this writing he is three years and seven months old . . . About two months ago his mother noticed for the first time that apparently he has colored hearing. Their home is not far from a rifle range, and the sound of the guns resounds through the hills with a loud 'boom'. One day Edgar asked: 'What is that big black noise?' A few days later he was being put to bed on the sleeping porch. Two crickets were chirping loudly, one of them having the usual cricket-sound with which he is familiar, the other having a very high, shrill chirp in comparison. He asked: 'What is that little white noise?' When his mother told him that it was a cricket he was not satisfied, and he said: 'Not the brown one, but the little white noise.' Then he imitated both of them, calling the lower brown and the shriller of the two white. At another time, when a cricket-chirp uttered from farther away came with a resonant buzz, he called it red. He calls the sound of the cicada white. The electric fan is orange, and the electric cleaner which has a deep 'burr' is black. The sound of a frog, neither very high nor very low, is bluish. (Reprinted from Whitchurch, A.K. (1922). Synaesthesia in a child of three and a half years. *American Journal of Psychology*, *33*, 302–303.)

The colorful albino

In 1812, George Sachs submitted a medical dissertation in the German university town of Erlangen that described his own remarkable condition. Sachs was an albino. His hair and skin were of purest white, as were those of his youngest sister. He had been born in Saint Ruprecht, a small and lonely village in a mountainous area, and was the oldest of five children. He was a religious and modest man with a high educational level. At this point in time, albinism had mainly been documented in Africa, where a white-skinned baby born to black parents would be treated as a monster, and barred from breeding. During the slave trade, these black albinos were sometimes acquired as curiosities to serve in the mansions and palaces of Europe. The great showman, Phineas Barnum, would later include albinos in his travelling circus. Our colorful albino, George Sachs, was 'discovered' by Dr Julius Schlegel in August 1795 at the age of nine. We know little of their relationship but Schlegel and Sachs would go on to become colleagues and, indeed, one of Schlegel's motivations for advancing Sachs was to prove that an albino can have a normal intellect, and could even practice as a doctor. Albinism is now understood in terms of genetic mutations in the proteins that make skin pigmentation and there is no logical reason why this would affect intellect. However, the story in this book is not concerned with the outward manifestations of color such as the color of our skin or hair. It concerns how some people color their *mental* worlds. Indeed, George Sachs was remarkable for another reason.

Towards the end of his medical dissertation, Sachs describes how certain sounds, words and ideas have colors that are not seen by the other people around him. In the alphabet, the letters A and E are both shades of red; I is white, as are M and N; D is yellow; S is dark blue and so on. Of the numbers, 1 is white, 2 is of uncertain color, 3 is ash color, 4 is red and so on. Groups of numbers took on the color of the last digit. So, for example, 34 and 24 are the color of four (= red) and 35 and 25 are the color of five (= yellow). Musical sounds also had colors, as did certain words such as city names and days of the week. The colors for these words did not always correspond to the colors of the letters that comprise them.

There is a certain irony in the fact that someone with such rich experiences of color was, in terms of physical appearance, devoid of color. Sachs' description is now recognized as the first medical account of the condition that we now know as synesthesia. I use the term 'condition' deliberately but with qualification. Synesthesia is a real phenomenon with a biological basis that is found in a minority of people. It is not, however, a disorder. Nor is it a condition that requires treatment or sympathy. It is not, with the benefit of hindsight, associated with albinism (most synesthetes are not albinos). In fact, synesthesia is a condition that many people aspire to. Many artists seek to recreate it. Many cultures induce it using 'magical' plants to achieve spiritual enlightenment. Having synesthesia may also lead to certain benefits in everyday life, such as to one's memory. This book tells the story of synesthesia and, in so doing, reveals important conclusions concerning how all of our brains create sensory experiences. How is it possible to experience color when there is no color there? What makes people with synesthesia different? Why might all babies be synesthetic? Why might sensory mixing be an important feature of all brains, whether synesthetic or not? Before going on to consider these questions, the first question that needs to be tackled is: what is synesthesia?

Aliens in the family

People with synesthesia experience the ordinary world in extraordinary ways. Words can have tastes; names can have color; and the sequence of numbers may glide through space. Most definitions of synesthesia emphasize that there is an 'extra' sensation that is tagged on to what would normally be expected. For example, the sound of a flute may be a pastel lemon color. The sound is both heard and seen, but the color does not replace the heard sound – it coexists with it. This is why synesthesia is regarded as an extra sensation. Of course, for someone with synesthesia it doesn't feel like there is something extra because they have experienced the world this way for all their life. On the contrary, to a synesthete, it seems like there is something *absent* in the experiences of the people around them. To a synesthete, the color of a musical note may be just as much of a property of the music as the note's pitch and it doesn't feel, to them, like it is extra. The New York artist, Carol Steen, describes it in the following way:

There have been times when I have had one sensation such as toothache and observed the color of the pain, its taste and smell. All these synesthetic perceptions are aspects of one overall experience. I perceive them as related in the same way that windows, a door and front steps combine to become the image of a house.

Synesthetes can always vividly remember the moment in their life that they discovered that their way of experiencing the world was fundamentally different from the people around them. It is fascinating that this insight into their own experiences comes about only by contrasting it with what other people claim to experience. We just take our experiences for granted unless they are questioned in some way. When revealed to be different they can suddenly take on an importance that they never previously enjoyed. One of our research volunteers, Debbie, describes the moment that she inadvertently ventured out of the synesthesia closet.

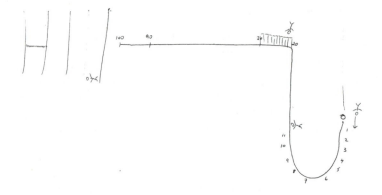

Figure 1 Debbie experiences numbers arranged in space, and she can vary the perspective from which her 'number form' is viewed. Each number would also have its own unique color to her.

I did not 'discover' my synesthesia until I made a comment to my parents in my mid-twenties about a number. They were disputing some number that I had given them as a statistic and I said, by way of proof, that it could not have been seventy and had to be forty because it was a red number with a warm feel, and it was only halfway up the line to 100. It is extremely strange when the two people who know you better than anyone else regard you as though you were a complete alien. I then went on to describe how my numbers are not only colored, but also have very distinct patterns, as does time – the time of day, days of the week, months within the year, and the years themselves.

Debbie's drawing of her arrangement of numbers in space is shown in Figure 1. She is able to vary the perspective from which the pattern is observed, and this is illustrated by the different positions of the 'little men'. Each number would also have a color.

The colors that people experience tend to be very precise and they rarely seem to change over time. The synesthetic color doesn't override the true color. They seem to coexist and compete for attention. The colors and the experiences are very hard to put into words. Some synesthetes see the color as if it is on the page, but they still claim to be able to see that the text is truly black and white. Others describe the colors on some kind of 'inner screen' or perhaps floating in space at a fixed distance from their body. I received the following email from a synesthete, Rosemary, after she had listened to a radio documentary about synesthesia. This was one of the very first times that she had attempted to put her own experiences into words.

I read in black and white and THINK in color. The word 'Scotland', for instance, is visible to my eyes as black, but is sensed as color in my head. I sense 'Scotland' spelled out in my head and the initial letter, S, lends an overall color to the feel of the whole word. In Scotland's case, gloss white, whilst the colors of the remaining seven letters are less significant and trail off into the distance. I've found it so hard to name colors. Words appear to be the wrong medium for what my brain 'sees' and 'feels'. For instance, after listening to your radio programme I at first thought of one of the brightest letters of the alphabet – the letter Q. I asked myself 'what color is Q'? The first answer I came up with was that 'Q was Q-colored'. I then realized this was nonsense, that Q wasn't a color; Q was an intense shade of pink. But 'pink' sounded totally wrong to me as the word 'pink' is composed of four colors beginning with brown (brown being the color of the letter P in 'pink'). Next I wondered why Q was pink, and straight away got the answer that Q was pink because queens were pink, but immediately realized that this was nonsense too – 'why are queens pink?' (the word 'queen' is probably pink because the letter Q is pink, but that doesn't help either). Next, I thought of the letter S, which is gloss white and, asking myself 'why', I assumed it was because snakes were white! Again, nonsense.

Synesthetes will often name their children to fit their synesthesia and choose their partners on this basis. This quote from one of our synesthetes, Sharon, is typical:

I was thinking the other day about my son's name [Adam]. It is red and yellow like mine. My husband's name is yellow. There are other names that I considered for my son but in the end I found I just couldn't have a child with a blue or purple name. It would feel like having a stranger in the family.

Synesthesia runs in families, so there is a strong likelihood that the child will have synesthesia themselves, but the child will probably associate a different color to the name, and – worse still – there is no guarantee that the color will be nice. One synesthete changed the spelling of her name from Sarah to Cera because the combination of colors in her original name clashed. Anne does not like the grayness of her name, as she explains:

I don't like my name because it is gray and olive green [a = gray but n = olive green], although the red-orange 'e' at the end makes it a little better. It still reminds me of those Spanish stuffed olives with a red-orange pimento. As the color of names go, it is not great.

When some people tell their parents that the number forty is 'red with a warm feel', they get quite a different response to that experienced by Debbie. 'No! Forty is dark green with a brittle feel' or 'No! Forty is a mixture of brilliant yellow for the 4 and translucent for the 0.' Although synesthesia runs in families, different family members disagree about what the 'correct' color is. George Sachs' youngest sister had synesthesia too, and they disagreed over the colors. I have come across a set of identical twins, Jacqueline and Mary, with similar types of synesthesia but different sets of colors. They hadn't discussed it together as children and they didn't even realize that their way of seeing the world was special until they were in their early twenties when one of them happened to mention it to her mother who regarded it as 'weird'. As Mary puts it:

I don't think I had even realized that my twin had it as well until then. We certainly argue about what colors certain letters are – I really can't imagine that she sees A as red, for example, whereas I see it as green. We have never come to blows over this. I suppose it is something that has made us a bit closer as it is something we share although in a slightly different way.

The first letters of their alphabets are given below.

	Jacqueline	Mary
A	red	light green
B	deep blue	indigo
C	yellow	dark violet
D	brown	dark brown
E	blue/black	very dark turquoise
F	pale mauve	lilac
G	brown, slightly golden	reddish brown
H	very pale blue	mustard yellow
I	pale gray/white	black

The fact that synesthesia runs in families doesn't automatically make it genetic. Money runs in families too, but wealth isn't genetic. However, there is scientific evidence of a genetic link to synesthesia. If synesthesia was inherited culturally by, for example, a mother teaching her daughter the colors of the alphabet then we would expect close agreement between mothers' and daughters' colors, or between the colors of pairs of siblings. This is not found. Many family members aren't even aware of each other's synesthesia until after childhood. Colored alphabet books have also been suggested to be involved, but this doesn't explain why some people exposed to these books develop synesthesia and others do not. A large survey of synesthetes in Australia compared their colors with those found in colored alphabet books published between 1914 and 1986, and found no evidence of any correspondence. Although synesthetic experiences of color are particularly common, synesthesia can be found for the other senses and different types of synesthesia can co-occur with a family. James Wannerton, whom we will meet again in Chapter 2, experiences tastes for words. For example, 'profit' tastes of unripe, pithy orange and 'peace' tastes of tomato soup. His sister reports a completely different type of synesthesia. When she reads, she experiences colored letters but the colors appear to be shining through the page. Synesthetes also often have more than one type of synesthesia. This suggests that different types of synesthesia have a common cause. Carol Steen, for example, experiences colors and other aspects of vision from touch, smell, sound, taste and pain. The albino, George Sachs, also had a wide variety of different types. All these facts argue against the view that synesthesia clusters in families because of word of mouth. But these facts also provide some clues as to how the gene is operating. The gene cannot determine exactly what types of synesthesia will be found in a person or what the precise associations will be (e.g. is 'A' red or light green?), but it does seem to increase the likelihood that they will develop some form of synesthesia.

Recent research has started collecting DNA samples from people with synesthesia and their relatives. Cells containing DNA can easily be obtained by gently rubbing the inside of one's cheek and the cell samples can be sent to laboratories in other parts of the world. Geneticists in Dublin (Ireland), Cambridge (UK) and Texas (USA) are currently hunting the synesthesia gene. This research has demonstrated, definitively, that there is a genetic component to synesthesia. However, it is looking less likely that there will be a single synesthesia gene. There may be several genes that are implicated in synesthesia. Perhaps different families have different synesthesia genes, or perhaps there are ten synesthesia genes and a person needs a certain number of these to become synesthetic. At present, we just don't know.

Is it possible to carry the synesthesia gene (or genes) but not be synesthetic? Yes. There are many cases of synesthesia, such as Debbie's, in which neither parent has synesthesia. Unless there is an unusually high incidence of synesthesia in milkmen (or mailmen in the US), it is likely that one or both parents could carry the gene without having synesthesia. Synesthesia has also been noted to skip generations such that grandparents and grandchildren have it but the intermediate generation does not. There are even some genetically identical twins in which one twin has it and the other one does not. This doesn't disprove a genetic theory, but it does prove that genes aren't everything. It is possible that both twins could have the synesthesia gene but only one goes on to develop synesthesia. The real test of the genetic theory lies in the twins' offspring. If both twins have the gene, then the non-synesthetic twin should be just as likely to have synesthetic children as the synesthetic twin. This remains to be seen. Ultimately, any explanation of synesthesia will have to address genetic and non-genetic influences. All the descriptions, so far, speak of synesthesia as a lifelong condition that people are born with. However, there are other types of synesthesia that have different causes. In subsequent sections and chapters, I will discuss how synesthesia can sometimes be triggered by the onset of blindness or can be temporarily induced by drugs such as LSD. Both of these examples illustrate that non-genetic factors need to be considered in a theory of synesthesia.

Vision, and color in particular, is by far the most common synesthetic experience relative to touch, taste, smell and hearing. However, there are many, many types of synesthesia and we shall encounter them throughout this book. One challenge for explaining synesthesia is to offer a satisfactory account of this diversity. Sean Day runs a synesthesia discussion forum (the 'synlist') and compiles a list of different types of synesthesia. Perhaps the most bizarre type on his list is 'colored orgasms'. This is found in one percent of people with synesthesia (note: not one percent of the whole population). One lady who sent me a sheepish email spoke of seeing something like her own private 'firework display' at the critical moment. I do not know whether synesthetic men can experience anything similar.

Carol Steen reports synesthetic sensations in response to touch and pain, and she uses her synesthetic experiences induced by acupuncture as inspiration for her art.

Lying there, I watched the black background become pierced by a bright red color that began to form in the middle of the rich velvet blackness. The red began as a small dot of color and grew quite large rather quickly, chasing much of the blackness away. I saw green shapes appear in the midst of the red color and move around the red and black fields.

One of the synesthetes that I have encountered, Rolf, experiences colors from smells. The color envelops him like a mist – 'A smell to me is more than a scent. I don't know how to write about it – it's almost like the bits in "Lord of the Rings" where Frodo puts the ring on!'

Everyone knows a synesthete, but not everyone knows that they know a synesthete. And they may not know who the synesthete is. When I have given lectures about synesthesia to audiences of scientists, many will still leave the lecture hall skeptical about whether it really exists. (Scientists are born skeptical.) They may then discuss this crazy lecture with their partner, family, friends or colleagues and, sure enough, someone will say 'hang on a minute, that's me!' It is as if meeting a living, breathing synesthete provides the evidence that no amount of hard science can, especially if that person is one of your trusted acquaintances. The anthropologist Robin Dunbar has argued that the human brain has a capacity to maintain about 150 active social relationships. If we work from this figure, then I estimate that we will all closely know around six or seven people who experience a type of synesthesia involving one of the five classical senses (vision, hearing, touch, taste, smell). There are likely to have been two British prime ministers and two American presidents with synesthesia (don't ask me who). The figure will be higher if we consider people outside of our immediate sphere (friends we no longer keep in touch with, friends of friends, etc.) and it will be higher still if we extend our search to other types of synesthesia, such as experiencing number or time as arranged in space.

In order to find out how common synesthesia is, we conducted an experiment on passers-by at London's Science Museum, and my colleague Julia Simner conducted a similar study on the undergraduate population in Edinburgh, Scotland. As well as asking people whether they experienced color when they saw, heard or thought about letters and numbers, we also devised a computer test in which black letters and numbers were flashed on the screen and people had to choose a color as quickly as possible. Most people chose randomly but those with synesthesia were very reliable in their choice of colors. This enabled us to estimate that this type of synesthesia occurred in one to two percent of the population. A similar result was found in Edinburgh, and the Edinburgh study was also able to consider other types of synesthesia. Colored days of the week were more common that we had originally expected, but we were able to observe less common types such as tasting shapes, and colored music. In total, we were able to identify 22 synesthetes out of 500 students who were initially screened.

Several famous individuals are known to have had synesthesia. Vladimir Nabokov, the author of *Lolita*, had it, as did his son, Dimitri, his mother, and his wife. He describes his colored letters in very precise terms. He notes that the combination of seven letters 'kzspygv' creates the rainbow of colors from violet through to red!

In the green group, there are alder-leaf f, the unripe apple of p, and pistachio t. Dull green, combined somehow with violet, is the best I can do for w. The yellows comprise various e's and i's, creamy d, bright-golden y, and u. In the brown group, there are the rich rubbery tone of soft g, paler j, and the drab shoelace of h.

The Nobel prize winning physicist Richard Feynman also saw letters in colors.

When I see equations, I see the letters in colors – I don't know why. As I'm talking, I see vague pictures of Bessel functions from Jahnke and Emde's book, with light tan j's. Slightly violet-bluish n's, and dark brown x's flying around . . . And I wonder what the hell it must look like to the students.

The philosopher Ludwig Wittgenstein may also have had colored letters. In his miscellaneous notes, he muses on the following: 'It's just like the way some people do not understand the question "What color has the vowel A for you?"'

This, of course, implies that Wittgenstein *does* know the color of the vowel A, which makes him a likely candidate for having synesthesia.

The rise and fall of synesthesia

George Sachs would never have bothered to describe his own synesthesia had it not been for a book published by one of his countrymen some two years earlier; namely Goethe's *Theory of Colors*, published in 1810. Johann Wolfgang von Goethe is to German literature as Dante and Shakespeare are to Italian and English literature. Although it is his works of fiction and poetry that earned him lasting fame and respect, Goethe himself was most proud of his foray into science: 'I am not too proud of my achievements as a poet . . . But that I am the only one in my century who knows the truth about the theory of colors – that is which I am proud of and which gives me a feeling of superiority over many!' Although his theory has never been taken seriously by scientists, his basic idea that we can understand color through biology rather than physics was surprisingly modern. It also went against the dominant view of the time, which was based on the physics of Isaac Newton. Newton had shown that a prism could be used to separate colorless light into the spectrum and, hence, that color is a property of light. Although he had no knowledge of synesthesia, Newton also speculated (incorrectly) that there might be a physical law linking the seven colors of the spectrum and the seven intervals on the Western musical scale. In contrast, Goethe argued that many aspects of color could not be explained by the physics of light. For example, if you stare at a green object and then look away you might see a red after-image. There is a famous image of the American flag in green, black and yellow. Stare at it for long enough and then look away at a white wall and you will see the image in red, white and blue. This occurs not because of the physical properties of light but because of the biology of our sensory apparatus. There are cells in our eyes and brain that respond maximally to red and minimally to green, and vice versa, that give rise to this illusion. In associating his synesthesia with Goethe rather than Newton, Sachs had made a wise move. It is indeed possible to experience red without the corresponding wavelength of light being present, as in the American flag afterimage. However, Sachs made a fundamental mistake that would take another fifty years to correct, namely the notion that synesthesia is a product of the eyes rather than the brain.

The case of George Sachs first appeared in a medical encyclopedia in 1814. The interest in this fascinating case lead to his dissertation, originally published in Latin, being translated into German in 1824 by his 'discoverer' Julius Schlegel. However, no new cases of synesthesia were documented until 1849 following a review of Sachs' case by Dr Edward Cornaz. Cornaz was the first person to give it a name: 'hyperchromatopsia'. His choice of name reflected his belief that the colors were originating from in the eye. He regarded synesthesia to be the opposite of color blindness, which is caused by a deficiency in a certain type of cell in the retina and prevents people from telling particular colors apart, usually red and green. Cornaz suggested that synesthetes have extra types of cell that create colors in situations where others cannot see them. It is interesting to note that these earliest explanations of synesthesia did not regard it as a disorder. If anything, it was viewed as a positive ability that reflects some higher refinement of our sense of seeing.

By the 1860s and 1870s a steady stream of new cases were being reported and the tide was turning; the eye was finally out and the brain was in. However, opinion was divided between two rival theories: those who believed that synesthesia was due to learned associations and those who believed that it reflected the way that nerves from different senses were interconnected. For example, Dr Kaiser (in 1872) was one of the first people to suggest that the colors for letters and words originate as a deliberate memory aid in childhood that then become spontaneously fixed throughout life. Others suggested more subtle forms of memory association: 'D is associated in my mind with dog, and when I think of a dog it never is a white dog, but always a black one;

hence, D is black.' Those who appealed to the linkage of the sensory nerves likened synesthesia to sensory reflexes such as sneezing when encountering a bright light, or chills when hearing a blackboard scratched.

In the 1880s and 1890s synesthesia had a golden age. Literally hundreds of cases were documented and synesthesia was a serious topic of investigation for some of the most eminent minds of that time. In Germany, Eugene Bleuler had a synesthetic student, Karl Lehmann, and together they reported 76 people (out of 596) who had vowel–color associations. Bleuler himself was a very influential figure who would later go on to study and name another very different neurological condition: schizophrenia.

In Britain, Charles Darwin's cousin, Sir Francis Galton, was interested in applying his cousin's theory of evolution to mental traits such as the vividness of mental images and the nature of genius. He was intrigued by the fact that synesthesia tended to run in families. However, his observation that women and children tended to have much stronger visual images then men led him to be skeptical of the possibility that this could contribute to a superior intellect! Many of his 'genius' respondents did not appear to think visually at all, as illustrated in one of the following quotes from a gentleman who returned his questionnaire unanswered:

These questions presuppose assent to some sort of a proposition regarding the 'mind's eye' and the 'images' which it sees . . . This points to some initial fallacy . . . It is only by a figure of speech that I can describe my recollection of a scene as a 'mental image' which I can 'see' with my 'mind's eye' . . . I do not see it . . . any more than a man sees the thousand lines of Sophocles which under due pressure he is ready to repeat.

For many people, including those with synesthesia, the idea of 'seeing' a 'mental image' with their 'mind's eye' is not a figure of speech but an accurate description of their sensory world.

In the USA, Mary Calkins conducted an extensive survey of synesthesia and, indeed, used 'that word' for the first time in an English publication. The word 'synesthesia' had been used since classical times to refer to phenomena such as referred pain in which, for instance, damage to the spine might be felt as pain on the knee (rather than pain on the spine). The term had been reintroduced in the nineteenth century, but Calkins was one of the first people to advocate its usage in the present context. Calkins would go on to become the first president of the American Psychological Association and was the first woman to study for a PhD at Harvard (although the degree was never awarded because she was a woman). Her investigations of synesthesia would have taken place while she was being tutored by William James who, along with Sigmund Freud, was the most eminent psychologist of his day. However, the love affair between science and synesthesia would not last. Within the next 50 years it would disappear from the scientific agenda as fast as it had arisen.

So why did synesthesia disappear off the scientific radar? Although studies of the brain continued apace throughout the twentieth century, the study of the mind (in psychology) took a rather different turn. During the mid-twentieth century, human behavior was understood by analogy to animal behavior. This approach was championed by people such as the Harvard professor B.F. Skinner and his so-called behaviorist colleagues. Typical experiments would involve rats in a box (a 'Skinner box') that are trained to press a lever when they encounter a sound or light, and are then given food rewards or electric shocks to modify their behavior. Skinner even developed a similar set-up for his daughter's crib that was commercially manufactured to help with the raising of babies, although minus the electric shocks. There are several reasons why an interest in synesthesia was incompatible with this approach. Firstly, psychology had become the 'science of behavior' rather than the 'science of the mind'. People with synesthesia do not behave differently from other people (you can never really tell if someone is synesthetic unless you ask them) and so there was no outward behavior that needed to be studied or explained. The fact that synesthetes claim to have very different ways of experiencing the world was considered irrelevant or trivial. Skinner and colleagues also believed that different minds reflected different environments rather than different genes. Although the existence of synesthesia was not necessarily denied, it was presumed to reflect the fact that some people must have been exposed to, say, a blue number '5' or heard a particular instrument in a red-colored room rather than a preexisting genetic disposition.

There is clearly a difference between somebody who has learned to say 'blue' when they hear the number '5' and somebody who sees a dark velvety blue shape 60 centimetres from their face when they hear the number '5'. These differences were not considered relevant by Skinner and his behaviorists and it would take until modern times before science decided that it could (and should) attempt to explain them. The nineteenth-century researchers of synesthesia, prior to Skinner, had already realized that there was something interesting to be explained but science wasn't ready to give them the explanation.

This book will unravel an account of synesthesia based on contemporary research. In doing so, we will have to reflect more carefully on our own sensory experiences of the world and be open to the possibility that our way of sensing the world is just one of many. In the next section, I will consider how we can experience color when no color is present and, indeed, how it is possible for some blind people to experience vision from their other senses. This will provide us with the first piece of the jigsaw in explaining synesthesia.

Can a blind man hear scarlet?

The experiences of the blind have intrigued and puzzled scientists for centuries. In the seventeenth century, the British philosopher John Locke (1632–1704) presented two puzzles concerning the nature of blindness and the nature of our sensory experiences. The first puzzle was suggested to him by William Molyneux, an Irish lawyer and Member of Parliament, and has therefore been dubbed 'Molyneux's question'. The question is as follows: can a man blind from birth, on recovering the use of his sight, correctly name a sphere and a cube that have been placed before his eyes? That is, can his existing ability to name these objects by touch be used to inform his vision when he sees them for the first time? The answer, according to these two thinkers, was 'no' – he would not be able to name them. Before I go on to explain their reasoning, let me introduce the second puzzle as it is clearly related to the first and is more closely related to synesthesia. Locke asks whether it is possible for a man, blind from birth, to understand what the color scarlet is like. He introduces the example of a 'studious' blind man for whom the sound of a trumpet was said to be scarlet. Some have interpreted this as an early reference to synesthesia, appearing over 120 years before George Sachs. This is not so. The case is a hypothetical example, and Locke clearly believes that it is impossible to experience color by any means other than vision. He argues that the blind man could use the word 'scarlet' to describe things, if he so fancied, but he could never really understand what scarlet was without having seen it.

Locke based his answers to these two puzzles on his intuitions rather than scientific observation. On reflection, his answers were half right and half wrong. Contrary to Locke, there are cases of blind synesthetes who report colors from spoken words, sounds and touch. Thomas Cutsforth was a blind psychology student at the University of Oregon in the 1920s. When he was reading Braille the colors of the letters appeared under his finger tips. It is to be noted that he wasn't seeing the actual color of the letters, but rather his own synesthetic colors for each letter. When counting, he experienced numbers arranged in space about 1 metre from his face with each number colored: 1 was white, 2 was dull gray tinged with yellow, 3 was reddish, and so on. When given a large number his eyes shifted to the right even though they could not see, and the numbers weren't really there to be seen.

Thomas Cutsforth and recent cases of synesthesia in the blind all had some vision before they became blind. He also had synesthesia before becoming blind. Is it possible to be blind from birth (i.e. congenitally blind) and experience synesthetic colors from sound or touch? This is impossible to know because these blind people would never develop the appropriate words to describe colors. It is logically conceivable that a blind person could experience colors from sound, but they would have no idea that color was normally a property of vision rather than a property of sound unless they had some experience of what vision was like. As such a congenitally blind synesthete, if such a person existed, would never think of their sensations as being unusual and would never come to our attention. Locke was correct to say that a congenitally blind person could never accurately use the word 'scarlet' to denote a sound, but he may have been wrong to assume that such a person could have no visual experience at all. As I will discuss later, blind people can use the visual parts of their brain for hearing and touch but what they actually experience is harder to know.

What of Molyneux's question? Are there instances of blind people who have recovered their sight that can instantly name all the objects around them? William Cheselden reported a case to the Royal Society in 1728, some years after Locke's death. The boy in question was about 13 or 14 years old and had recovered sight following a cataract operation. Cheselden reports the following:

At first the boy was unable to name anything he saw, but apparently he could distinguish shapes, for he was easily able to learn their names. In order to learn the difference between a cat and a dog, he handled the cat, looked at it intently and then said 'So puss! I shall know you another time.'

This example appears to support Locke's answer to the question: the blind man would only be able to name the cat from sight after the knowledge had been transferred from his sense of touch. However, Locke's reasoning was not wholly accurate. He had assumed that once sight was restored then vision would be instantly normal, rather than more accurate situation that the brain must somehow learn how to see. There are also more recent cases such as that of Sydney Bradford, reported in 1963, that point to an opposite conclusion. Bradford was blind from birth but received a cornea transplant at 52 years of age. He was reported to have immediate vision for objects already known to him by touch. In Chapter 2, I shall point out that babies who also have to learn how to see show a remarkable ability to transfer information across the senses.

Most people might imagine blindness and deafness to be the same as our own experiences of darkness and silence. They are not. Fully sighted people do not have 360 degree vision but the parts of space that we can't see are not sensed as dark, they just don't exist as any kind of visual experience (light, dark or whatever). Now try to imagine that vision doesn't exist in any part of space. This may come close to the experiences of the blind, or at least the congenitally blind. The congenitally blind inhabit a world in which certain concepts can be hard to grasp fully. The philosopher Denis Diderot describes a conversation with a blind man about his understanding of mirrors and other optical devices. Although he has felt the smooth surface of a mirror, and has been told that the mirror can create a duplicate impression of an object, he fails to comprehend fully why the duplicate itself cannot be touched. He asks other curious questions about optical devices that he had never before encountered; for example, whether magnifying devices were larger than those that reduced the apparent size of objects.

All this discussion is focused on blindness being a deficit, but there is a flip side to this. Blind people appear to have more finely tuned other senses, particularly hearing and touch. In the days when everyone had a piano in their home, blind piano-tuners were common and highly respected. John Hull in his book *Touching the Rock: An Experience of Blindness* describes how he gradually loses the ability to think and remember visually in the years following the onset of his blindness. But in doing so, his other senses take on a richness that they never had before. For instance, thunder

gives a sense of space and distance. Thunder puts a roof over my head, a very high, vaulted ceiling of tumbling sound. I realize that I am in a big place, whereas before there was nothing at all. The sighted person always has a roof overhead in the form of the blue sky or the clouds, or the stars at night. The same is true for the blind person of the sound of the wind in the trees. It creates trees; one is surrounded by trees whereas before there was nothing.

It is not at all surprising that blind people would rely more on their other senses. However, the mechanism by which they do so is quite remarkable. In sighted people, inputs from the eye send signals to regions of the brain that are specialized for vision. Similarly, information from our other sense organs relay signals to their own specialized regions in the brain. This leads us to an intriguing question: what happens to the visual regions of the brain when the eye is damaged and is unable to stimulate it? There is now convincing evidence to suggest that the parts of the brain normally dedicated to vision get 'taken over' by the senses of hearing and touch. Brain imaging has shown that when blind people read Braille by touch, the parts of the brain normally dedicated to vision become activated. The same happens when blind people are required to determine where in the room a sound is located. Blind people literally hear and touch by using parts of the brain that, under normal circumstances, would support vision. But in this situation does touch feel like touch, or does it feel like vision? Or does touch feel like touch plus vision? Does sound feel like sound, does it feel like vision, or does it feel like sound plus vision? We can't ask these questions to a congenitally blind person because they don't know what vision feels like. In most blind people with previous visual experience, sound feels like sound and touch feels like touch. However, a few people do report that sounds can feel like sound plus vision and touch can feel like touch plus vision. That is, the sensory reorganization that takes place after losing vision can result in someone becoming synesthetic who was not previously synesthetic. One person, recently described by researchers in Oxford, became blind after a car accident had damaged his optic nerves. About a year after the accident he noticed that loud and unexpected sounds produced flashes of light. We do not know why synesthesia arises in some people but not others after they become blind. Perhaps some people have a greater propensity for sensory reorganization than others. Perhaps it is actually far more common than we realize because people might worry about reporting these symptoms to a doctor in case it looks like hallucinations or madness.

There is evidence to suggest that this kind of sensory reorganization can occur quickly. Alvaro Pascual-Leone and colleagues conducted an experiment in which normally sighted university students were completely blindfolded for several days. Most of them reported that they started 'seeing things' and some of these visions were synesthetic in nature. One participant reported flashing lights when listening to TV and another reported seeing a ghostly trail of light when her arm was moved in front of her.

There is, of course, another way for those who weren't born with synesthesia to experience such things. This is through hallucinogenic drugs such as LSD (or 'acid'), mescaline and magic mushrooms. Albert Hoffmann, the chemist who accidentally discovered the hallucinatory effects of LSD, reported the following: 'It was particularly remarkable how every acoustic perception, such as the sound of a door handle or a passing automobile, became transformed into optical perceptions. Every sound generated a vividly changing image, with its own consistent form and color.'

The effects of these drugs on perception are profound and can occur within an hour. They occur so quickly that it is inconceivable that the brain could undergo a radical reorganization of the senses in that time. As such, it suggests that our senses are already intertwined and connected, and that the drug somehow unblocks these connections. Indeed, there is good evidence that our senses aren't as separate as you might think (even in fully sighted people). The psychedelic movement of the 1960s described it as 'tuning in' or as opening 'the doors of perception' in Aldous Huxley's famous account of his mescaline trip. The implication was that other sensory worlds already exist in our brains and are there to be discovered. In medical experiments, LSD was administered to blind participants, some of whom had lost their sight over 50 years before, and many of them reported temporary visual experiences. Of course they weren't able to see external objects but their brains were able to experience simple sensations of light and color that were perhaps triggered by thoughts or sounds.

There are more serious attempts at enabling blind people to see by virtue of their other senses. These are called 'sensory substitution devices'. Peter Meijer has developed software that converts visual images to sounds via a hidden camera mounted on the wearer's head. The blind person hears the visual image as a 'soundscape' scanned from a left to right direction, with high-pitched sounds denoting objects higher up in the image and loudness reflecting the brightness of the image. Pat Fletcher was one of the first users of the system almost 20 years after she had been blinded in an industrial accident. She describes how she had to learn how to interpret the soundscapes by moving known objects in front of the camera. She describes the moment while trying to learn how to interpret the sounds, when she first *saw* a new soundscape: 'For there in the middle of my study is what looked like a hologram image of the wall and the gate, and I thought: wow, this thing really works.'

She insists that it is like seeing and not like hearing, and thus represents an example of a man-made synesthesia. Her vision is solely dependent on sounds and the camera system that converts images to sounds. When the battery runs out in her camera, the sounds slur and fade, and so does her vision. She can't see in color and her vision lacks fine detail:

My vision is based on black and white and all the little gradients in between. The best way I try to describe it to people is: take a large black sheet of paper. Now take a magical piece of white chalk and sketch me . . . in a line drawing. Now make me three dimensional and you've just about represented how my sight looks.

Another type of sensory substitution device converts camera images to touch. Paul Bach-y-Rita developed arrays of tiny mechanical vibrators or electrical stimulators that are applied to the back, thigh or even the tongue and receive input from a hidden camera. Within a short amount of time of exploring with the camera, the sensation triggered by the device stops feeling like a purely tactile experience and is described in visual terms.

It goes without saying that not all people with synesthesia have problems with vision or their other senses. Nor are they all on LSD. Synesthesia appears to have several causes, including sensory loss, drug-induced forms, and a naturally occurring form such as that first reported in George Sachs. However, the discussion on blindness has highlighted some general principles that will play an important part in explaining *all* types of synesthesia. I have noted that there are parts of the brain that are specialized for vision. It is the stimulation of these parts of the brain, rather than stimulation of the eyes, that gives rise to our conscious experiences of seeing. For people who lose vision (e.g. in an accident that damages the eyes), the visual parts of the brain may start to be stimulated via other means. Other senses such as touch and hearing may activate these visual regions of the brain, giving rise, in some people, to visual hallucinations or synesthesia. People who were synesthetic prior to becoming blind can carry on seeing colors after blindness, as in the case of Thomas Cutsforth, who sees a colored sequence of numbers when he counts. We cannot be certain what people who are congenitally blind (i.e. from birth) actually experience, but we know that the visual regions of their brains are used by the other senses. In order to take us another step nearer to understanding synesthesia, I need to discuss one additional property of the visual regions of the brain: namely, the fact that different visual regions are specialized for different aspects of vision. In particular, there is one region of the brain that is specialized for color.

The early pioneers of synesthesia research had speculated on the existence of a 'chromatic center' in the brain (a region specialized for color), but the evidence for it was not widely accepted at that time. That evidence has emerged subsequently, and has been championed by the research of Semir Zeki and others. Zeki identified a region of the brain called V4 that responded specifically to color (the '4' refers to the fourth visual region; there is a V1, V2 etc.). This part of the brain appears to be active when we look at colored images but is not active when we look at the same image rendered in shades of gray. Area V4 is also related to our conscious perception of color, and our conscious experiences of color do not correspond faithfully to the wavelengths of light. For instance, the same physically identical color can be perceived either as orange or brown depending on whether the brain interprets it as lying in shadow or directly illuminated (for some examples see www.lottolab. org). Area V4 is responsible for this illusion. V4 infers the color of objects taking account of the surrounding lighting conditions. For example, it takes into consideration whether an object is in shadow or whether it is viewed under a bluish light.

If there are regions of the brain that are specialized for vision then it should be possible to go blind by damaging the visual parts of the brain, leaving the eye intact. This is in contrast to the more common example of blindness considered so far, i.e. damage to the eyes but an intact brain. Indeed this is so. Some people do become clinically blind after a stroke or head injury, despite having normally functioning eyes. However, damage to the visual regions of the brain very rarely leaves people completely blind. Some aspects of vision may remain intact while others are completely lost. For example, some very rare cases have damage to area V4, the color center of the brain. This produces a condition called cerebral achromatopsia in which people perceive the world normally but in shades of black and white. For other cases of cerebral achromatopsia colors are not completely absent but appear 'washed out' or 'dirty'. The eyes function normally and still detect different wavelengths of light, but the actual conscious experience of color is absent. It is very different to the example of 'color blindness' discussed earlier, which is related to the eyes and in which some colors (e.g. red and green) get confused. 'Color-blind' people still see the world in color (albeit fewer colors) whereas for the cerebral achromatopsic, the experience of color is absent altogether.

Oliver Sacks, in his book *An Anthropologist on Mars*, describes the case of Jonathan I. (or Mr I), a famous painter who acquired cerebral achromatopsia as a result of a car accident. His brown dog now looked dark gray. The dog would stand out sharply if it stood in direct sunlight, but in a half-shadow it could blend in with the background and almost disappear. It appeared so strange that he considered getting a Dalmatian. Tomato juice was black. At first, he would have to close his eyes to drink it. His own skin color and that of other people were a 'rat-colored' grey. Jonathan's art work had always been very colorful, so his brain damage changed his professional life completely. His attempts to continue painting in color were unsuccessful, and eventually he succumbed to the inevitable. He would paint in black and white. One of his first paintings was based on his experience of seeing a black and white sunrise. As he was unable to disentangle the various colors, the sunrise appeared like a slow nuclear explosion on the horizon as blacks gave way to whites. He wondered whether anyone had ever seen a sunrise this way before. Ironically, art critics who were unaware of his condition were enthusiastic about the 'creative renewal' in his artistic output. The case of Jonathan I. vividly illustrates how our conscious perception of color is tied to the brain and may be largely separable from other aspects of vision. However, there is another reason why the case is important. Prior to his car accident, Jonathan had synesthesia. After his accident the colors were gone from his synesthesia, just as they were gone from his external sight. Music no longer triggered sensations of color. We do not know much about his synesthesia, and I suspect that it did not disappear entirely. It is possible that music still evoked vision, but the vision itself would appear in shades of gray. Jonathan I. died in the late 1980s and it is doubtful that we will ever find such a rare case again.

In summary, although science largely abandoned synesthesia for almost 50 years, during this period important steps were made in understanding vision and color. The idea of other sensory worlds was kept alive during this period through explorations of sensory reorganization in blindness and through cultural awakenings in the use of hallucinogens such as LSD. It would only be a matter of time before synesthesia re-entered the scientific main-stream.

Not enough points on the chicken

The modern age of research into synesthesia began at a dinner party. The date was February 10 1980, and the venue was an artist's loft in suburban North Carolina. The host was Michael Watson and his guest was the flamboyant Dr Richard Cytowic. Cytowic tells the story as follows:

I sat nearby while he whisked the sauce he had made for the roast chickens. 'Oh dear,' he said, slurping a spoonful, 'there aren't enough points on the chicken.'

'Aren't enough what?' I asked.

He froze and turned red, betraying a realization that his first impression had been as awkward as that of a debutante falling down the stairs . . . 'Flavors have shape,' he started, frowning in to the depths of the roasting pan. 'I wanted the taste of this chicken to be a pointed shape, but it came out all round.' He looked up at me, still blushing. 'Well, I mean it's nearly spherical . . . I can't serve this if it doesn't have points.'

Further probing revealed that angostura bitters is 'an organic sphere . . . with tendrils. It has the springy con-sistency of a mushroom, almost round . . . but I feel bumps and can stick my fingers into little holes on the surface.' Michael sweeps his hands through the empty air and insists that he doesn't see anything. He *feels* it in his hands as if it were in front of him. As the flavor evolves on his tongue so does the shape in his hands which undergoes a metamorphosis of shape, size, weight, temperature and texture. The sensations are normally felt against his face or sitting in his hands.

When Richard Cytowic published his results in 1982 it was the first case report of synesthesia in 16 years (and that early report had appeared in a psychiatric journal, of all places). It was also one of few studies to conduct an

experiment of any sort rather than relying solely on observation. Cytowic gave Michael ten trials of ten liquid flavors
in a random order and asked him to choose the best answer
from an array of over 20 different shapes. Would he choose
the shapes in a random way, like most other people, or
would he choose them in an orderly way? Sure enough,
Michael tended to pick the same shape for the same tastes
in a non-random way and more simple tastes, such as salt,
were associated with fewer choices than more complex
tastes, such as angostura bitters.

A few years later and on the other side of the Atlantic,
Dr Simon Baron-Cohen flipped through the pages of the
Bulletin of the British Psychological Society. In it was an
advert placed by a 76-year-old painter, Elizabeth Stewart-
Jones, in which she described herself as 'An artist who has
experienced the lifelong condition of hearing words and
sounds in color'. Elizabeth was keen to learn more about
her condition and invited scientists to get in touch. Simon
Baron-Cohen took up the gauntlet and devised a simple but
effective way of showing that her synesthesia was more
than just spurious color associations that came to mind. For
Elizabeth each word had a very precise color, such that
Moscow was 'darkish gray, with spinach-green and pale
blue in places' and Daniel was 'deep purple, blue, and red,
and is shiny'. When she was unexpectedly asked ten weeks
later about the same words, she produced exactly the
same descriptions. Maybe she just has very good memory?
Indeed, we shall discuss later how synesthesia can be an
aid to memory. However, on standardized tests of memory
Elizabeth was unexceptional. Moreover, a much younger
person asked to generate color associations and recall them
after two weeks was only 17 percent consistent. Other cases
that came to the attention of Baron-Cohen would have
colors for each letter of the alphabet, and when they
listened to someone speaking they experienced colored
subtitles of the words spelled out. For example, a word like
'fish' might take on the green color of the letter 'f', and
'photo' might take on the lavender color of the letter 'p'.
This could even happen even though the 'f' and 'ph' sound
the same in 'fish' and 'photo'.

With the development of brain imaging techniques, it was going to be only a matter of time before synesthesia was put under the magnetic microscope. In functional MRI (magnetic resonance imaging), people place their heads (and brains) inside a harmless magnetic field that is around 10,000 times stronger than the earth's natural magnetic field. The machine produces loud clunking noises perhaps more reminiscent of a Heath Robinson invention than the state-of-the-art technology that it actually is. When the nerve cells in the brain are working they consume oxygen, and this produces changes in the amount of oxyhemoglobin and deoxyhemoglobin in the blood. These changes distort the magnetic field and enable researchers to figure out which parts of the brain are working the most (i.e. consuming the most oxygen) at a given point in time. Julia Nunn and her colleagues in London placed twelve synesthetes in the MRI scanner and observed what happened in their brains when they listened to speech. As with the synesthetes studied before, these people tended to see words in color. During the experiment they were blindfolded to ensure that they could not be literally seeing colors or seeing anything else. The results were very clear. These synesthetes activated the region of visual brain that is specialized for color, namely area V4. If area V4 is lost, as in the achromatopsic painter Jonathan I., then our experience of color is lost. If V4 is activated by a sense other than vision then this other sense is perceived as colored, as in the case of these 'colored hearing' synesthetes. What is particularly satisfying about this experiment is that the researchers also trained a group of control participants who lack synesthesia to associate colors with words. Thus, people would learn by rote that, say, 'photo' is lavender and 'fish' is green. In the scanner they would then be asked to recall or imagine the color. Again, synesthetes activated area V4 but control participants did not even when they had learned word–color associations. This provides the most convincing evidence against the long-standing suggestion that synesthesia is just learned color associations. Synesthetes claim to 'see' the colors and now science was in a position to say 'yes, you really do see colors'.

If someone in the street asks me what is the most convincing evidence that synesthesia is real, my answer is 'brain imaging'. It is true that these methods give synesthesia a level of credibility that it has never before enjoyed. However, it is probably not the main reason why synesthesia research is flourishing. Many scientists such as Simon Baron-Cohen and Richard Cytowic had accepted synesthesia as a legitimate line of research prior to the brain imaging studies. Moreover, the observations that led scientists in the 1980s and 1990s to believe in the existence of synesthesia were exactly the same as those made by scientists 100 years earlier, namely that synesthesia (a) tends to be very stable over time; (b) tends to run in families even though family members often disagree about the 'correct' colors; (c) tends to be very specific ('not any blue but that particular blue', etc.); and (d) occurs quickly. Even in the 1890s it had been observed that synesthetes were just as fast to say that the letter D is 'tan colored' as they were to say that the letter D is called 'dee'. In my opinion, it is the development of new *ideas* over the past century rather than the existence of new evidence or new techniques that brings the explanation of synesthesia within our grasp. We have learned so much about how the senses develop, how the senses interconnect in the brain, and how the brain gives rise to our conscious experiences of seeing, feeling, smelling, and so on. In the chapters that follow, I will unravel some of these issues in order to present my own theory about synesthesia.

This chapter has laid the foundations for understanding and explaining synesthesia. I have explained how our experiences of seeing depend on the functioning of our brain rather than just on our eyes. Parts of the brain dedicated to vision are normally activated by input from the eyes, but under some circumstances the visual parts of the brain may be activated from other regions of the brain. This can happen when we take drugs such as LSD, it can sometimes happen when our brains re-wire themselves to compensate for blindness, and it may happen as a result of a genetic difference in people who are born synesthetic. Within the visual regions of the brain there is an area called V4 that is specialized for color. When this region is lost, the world is seen in shades of gray. If V4 receives inputs from speech as well as vision, it may give rise to 'colored hearing' synesthesia. This is far from a full explanation of synesthesia. I haven't yet considered in any detail the other senses. I haven't considered why synesthetes have the particular associations that they do. Why do most synesthetes think that 'O' is white? Why colored letters at all? I haven't considered whether synesthesia is related to multisensory illusions that we may all experience from time to time.

Our colorful albino, George Tobias Ludwig Sachs, died shortly after his 28th birthday of something described as 'nerve fever' only two years after publishing his account of his albinism and his synesthesia. During his last few years he taught on topics such as medicine, pathology, and even astronomy, but his personal research interests had dealt with a topic closer to his heart – namely, the use of chemistry to further our understanding of color. Perhaps his genes and his synesthesia live on in his family's descendants. An interest in synesthesia is very much alive today and is leading us to re-evaluate how our brains create sensory experiences, and how information from our senses is linked together. This will be considered in the next chapter. Perhaps we all have more in common with the enigmatic world of synesthesia than you might think.

Counting on the senses

How many senses do we have? According to an article published in the January 2005 edition of *New Scientist*, the answer is 21. Or ten. Or 33. Or possibly three. But not, apparently, the five senses that we were taught in school – vision, hearing, touch, smell and taste. Where are these numbers coming from and why should it be a source of disagreement? Surely the number of senses that we have cannot be a matter of opinion; it must be answerable by science. However, for most scientists who study the senses this question is not seriously debated because the question itself is regarded as ambiguous or unanswerable. Even the *New Scientist* article concludes that 'senses may one day be consigned to the scientific dustbin'. In order to understand why it is hard, if not impossible, to count the senses, we will have to engage in a radical rethink of what our senses are, what they do, and how they work.

Our traditional Western view that there are five senses stems from the Greek philosopher, Aristotle. Aristotle lived in the fourth century BC. He was a tutor to Alexander the Great and a scholar of every subject imaginable at that time. Aristotle's views about science and medicine endured right up until the early nineteenth century, and some aspects of his science are still present in our everyday culture – including the notion that we have five senses. For Aristotle, each sense was linked to a sensory organ: the eyes for seeing, the nose for smelling, and so on. Bread may take on the smell of garlic if the two are left nearby, but it would be wrong to say that the bread had smelled the garlic. According to Aristotle, a sense of smell can only exist when it interacts with its appropriate sensory organ – the nose. This idea about the senses also led the seventeenth-century philosopher John Locke, whom we met in the first chapter, to claim that a blind man could never see the color scarlet from the sound of a trumpet, since color was associated with one particular organ (the eye).

Cultures that have never heard of Aristotle take a different view as to how many senses we have and what these senses are. For example, the Cashinahua of Eastern Peru have senses corresponding to skin knowledge, hand knowledge, eye knowledge, ear knowledge, genital knowledge and liver knowledge. It is also possible that non-human species have completely different senses. Pit-vipers have special organs underneath their eyes to detect infrared; bats detect ultrasound; certain fishes and turtles appear to navigate with magnetic fields; and a star-nosed mole has a fleshy, tendriled nose that could be used for detecting tactile objects, or chemical or electrical fields. It is not obvious whether this nose has any sensory similarity with our human nose.

So how did *New Scientist* magazine arrive at its answer, or answers? In order to answer the question 'how many senses do we [humans] have?' one needs to specify exactly what it is that is being counted. Is it the physical energies that give rise to sensation – light and so on? Is it the sensory organs, which Aristotle believed consisted of five? Is it the types of sensory receptors in the organs? For example, the retina of the eye has separate receptors for light and dark versus color. Is it the different sensory qualities of our experience that are being counted? For example, touch and temperature have very different qualities even though they are both sensed by the skin.

If our starting point is the number of types of physical energy, then we can count three human senses: light (vision), chemical (including taste and smell), and mechanical (including touch and hearing; note that sound waves mechanically oscillate hairs and membranes in the inner ear). Of course, Aristotle has already pointed out the problem with this approach: non-living matter can respond to light, chemical, and mechanical stimulation. For instance, we do not wish to say that bread is capable of smelling garlic, even though the two can interact chemically.

If we count the number of specialized cell receptors that respond to specific signals then this yields an answer between 21 and 33, depending on how they are counted. For instance, the retina contains two types of specialized cell that respond to light/dark or to color (making two visual senses) but the color receptors could be subdivided into three types (making four visual senses).

The approach that many scientists favor is actually not dissimilar to that originally taken by Aristotle, in that it considers the senses as systems rather than receptor types. The *New Scientist* estimate based on this approach yields the answer 'ten', and these are listed below. The list contains the 'famous five' together with three others that you should be familiar with (pain, temperature, and balance) and two that you have probably never given any thought about (proprioception and interoception):

1   vision
2   hearing
3   smell
4   taste
5   touch
6   pain
7   temperature
8   vestibular (balance)
9   proprioception (or 'mechanoreception': position and movement of joints and muscles)
10 interoception (internal sensation: hunger, heartbeat, bladder-stretch, etc.)

With your eyes closed, try moving your arm around in different positions. You can sense the position of the arm but you are not relying on any of your famous-five senses. You are relying on proprioception. Proprioception is based on receptors in the muscles and ligaments that are used to sense the position of the body in space. Professional dancers will make extensive use of this sense. Just as it is possible to lose our sense of vision and hearing through blindness and deafness, it is possible to selectively lose our less well-known senses. Oliver Sacks describes the case of Christina, the 'Disembodied Lady', who has no sense of her own body following a viral infection of her spinal cord. If she was carrying a briefcase it would literally fall out of her hands the moment she failed to attend to it, and she would have no sense of where her limbs were in space unless she looked at them. Gravity would pull her jaw agape unless she concentrated on keeping it closed. But this was not due to muscular weakness. It was due to a lack of sensory information about the current position of her jaw. She could feel physical sensations as well as before, suggesting that this really is different from the sense of touch and pain.

Interoception is defined as the 'sense of the physiological condition of the body'. It includes receptors that detect the stretch of the bladder (i.e. signaling the need to urinate), lung inflation, blood glucose levels (related to hunger), pH levels, and heartbeat. Some scientists would include pain and temperature here too, taking our number of senses back down to a more manageable eight.

Senses other than the famous five may participate in synesthesia, although they appear to be far rarer. I have come across one person who noticed, when doing yoga, that when her body was held in particular poses she experienced a dot of light that varied in color, size and texture. For instance, the 'mountain' position is an electric blue dot. This is a probable example of proprioception-color synesthesia. Examples of synesthesia involving pain are more common. Dudycha and Dudycha list the colors of eight different types of pain in their synesthete. Headaches are a dark blue spearhead sensation and numbness is a white prickly sensation. 'A dull, throbbing pain is seen as a large, brownish-purple globular figure resembling an ink blot . . . it is about four and one-half by six and one-half inches. This is most usually located in the abdomen.' Again, feelings of pain may be partially separable from touch. It is possible to feel pain from the stomach or the nerve of a tooth even though these parts of the body lack touch receptors.

Naturally occurring synesthesia involving interoception and the vestibular sense have not been documented before. Do synesthetes have colored balance, colored hunger or colored out-of-breathness? I know of one form of synesthesia that involves interoception, although it may only occur under the influence of drugs such as LSD. It is commonly reported that objects look as if they are 'breathing' after one takes this drug. A seen object may rhythmically expand and contract like it is inhaling and exhaling. For instance, one friend reported seeing a shelf of books breathing in and out like an accordion! What makes this experience potentially synesthetic in nature is that the book shelf was noted to be breathing in synchrony with his own respiration. That is, an aspect of interoception was projected into visual perception.

It is certainly true that some senses appear to participate in synesthesia more than others, but we don't know why. One possibility is that synesthesia is triggered by senses that are normally associated with high awareness. We are typically aware of vision, hearing, touch and taste but senses such as smell, balance, proprioception, and interoception tend to function with minimal awareness (and all these senses rarely participate in synesthesia). Another possibility that fits within the scope of this chapter is that some senses are more isolated from each other. For example, vision strongly influences the way that we hear and taste. Our sense of interoception, on the other hand, is more isolated from the other senses.

Specifying what it is that needs to be counted is one reason why the question (how many senses do we have?) lacks scientific rigor. But there is another deeper problem that potentially renders the question meaningless. In order to count things one needs to assume that they are separate entities. Clearly our eyes and ears are separate entities, but when sensory information arrives in the brain it ceases to be fully segregated. Our brains, and the nerve cells in them, pull together information from different senses and link it with our previous experiences of sensing the world. The radical rethink proposed in this chapter is that we can no longer think of our senses as separate entities that are potentially countable. This chapter will consider how our senses are linked together in the brain. I will demonstrate to you that the 'bizarre' condition of synesthesia is not a million miles away from what we all do, every minute of the day. I will discuss evidence to suggest that human infants experience a very different sensory world from the one that we inhabit, and I'll explain why we eat and drink with our eyes, and see through our ears.

The buzzing world of babies

The sensory receptors in our bodies (on the skin, retina, internal organs, and so on) are active in the womb and may be able to detect the sound of the mother's voice, her heartbeat, and the taste of the amniotic fluid. However, this does not mean that a baby, on being born to the world, will be capable of the same kinds of sensory experiences as you or me. A newborn must learn how to see, learn how to hear, learn how to taste, and so on. This consists of far more than just improving its ability to discriminate finer details or further distances. It involves learning that there is, in fact, a world 'out there' in which objects and other people exist. A newborn may have sensations of light, color, touch, smell, and so on, but they do not understand that there is a world that causes these sensations. A newborn lives in a private cocoon of sensations. The eminent psychologist, William James, described the world of the newborn as 'One great blooming, buzzing confusion'. At this point, it is important to understand that psychologists tend to make a distinction between 'sensation' and 'perception'. Our sensations are likened to our raw feel of something, such as a sensation of redness, whereas our perceptions are based on a comparison of current sensation with all previous sensations. Thus, perceiving a tomato involves more than sensing a red, round object; it also involves comparing it with our previous experience of seeing tomatoes. According to this division, a newborn has sensation but not perception. It is a 'blooming, buzzing confusion' because it struggles to make sense of its sensations. Learning about the senses effectively involves learning about cause and effect: for instance,

understanding that a sensation of lightness reflects someone peering into the crib or understanding that warmth is
due to the presence of a blanket.

Daphne and Charles Maurer have proposed an even
more radical view of what a newborn must learn. They
argue that a newborn doesn't just have to learn how to see
and how to hear; it has to learn that it has different senses
for seeing, hearing and so on. In answer to the question
'how many senses do we have?' their theory suggests that a
newborn has one. They argue that all human infants start
life with a form of synesthesia in which all the senses are
intermingled, and in which vision may be triggered by
hearing as well as sight, and so on. As they put it:

The newborn does not keep his sensations separate from one
another. He mixes sights, sounds, feelings, and smells into a
sensual bouillabaisse. Sights have sounds, feelings have tastes,
and smells can make him dizzy. The wildest of 1960s' psyche-
delia could not begin to compare with the everyday experience of a baby's entry into the world.

During development, an infant must learn to apportion
different sensations to different inputs. However, this is
only partially successful and we all, as adults, still possess
interlinked senses and remnants of the type of synesthesia
that we experienced in infancy.

What evidence is there to support the Maurers' idea
that we all start life as synesthetes? Of course it goes without saying that one important piece of evidence is lacking –
we can't directly ask newborns what they are experiencing.
Nevertheless, there are a wide variety of ways of studying
the newborn's sensory world and this does provide some
convincing evidence of a greater mixing of the senses in
infancy. First of all we can look at what happens inside the
brains of newborns. The nerve cells of the brain generate
tiny electrical fields when they are functioning. These
electrical 'brain waves' can be detected and amplified by
placing electrodes on the scalp. This doesn't harm the baby
as it is only recording what is naturally happening in their
brains. When an infant is played sounds it creates electrical

activity in the parts of the brain dedicated to hearing *and* the parts of the brain dedicated to vision. This is not found in older children or adults. It is as if a sound has visual as well as acoustic properties. Similarly, a touch applied to the baby's wrist generates electrical activity in the parts of the brain related to tactile perception. If the touch is accompanied by 'white noise' (like an untuned radio) then the brain's response is amplified. The same does not occur in adults. We cannot definitively conclude that the baby experiences synesthesia, but we can conclude that there is a far greater mixing of the senses in infancy than at other stages of life.

It is generally believed that babies require an optimal level of stimulation to regulate their sleeping and other early behaviors. Too much stimulation and the baby will be distressed (i.e. cry). Too little and the baby will try to seek out stimulating objects (e.g. looking at a mobile) or attract attention (i.e. cry). As any new parent will know, it is a tough and frustrating game trying to figure out whether the baby is crying because he/she needs more or less stimulation. According to Daphne Maurer, this may occur because stimulation from one sense (e.g. hearing) may feel like stimulation from any other sense (e.g. vision), and stimulation of lots of senses at the same time pushes the confusion through the roof. A study by David Lewkowicz and Gerald Turkewitz is consistent with this view. First of all, they got adults to match intensity levels of sounds and lights. A brighter light will be matched to a louder sound and so on. They then presented one-month-old babies with a white light on a number of successive occasions and monitored their pulse. After a while, the baby gets bored of the light (its pulse drops). This process is termed habituation. If the baby is then shown a light of a different intensity, its pulse will quicken. The crucial part of the experiment compares how the baby responds when a noise burst is substituted for a light. If the sound is of the same intensity as the light, will the baby treat them as if they are the same (i.e. its pulse remains constant or drops) or will it recognize that the noise is different to the light (i.e. the pulse will quicken)? They found that the babies respond to sounds and lights of the same intensity as if they are the same thing. This is consistent with Daphne Maurer's view that the newborn baby may perceive sound as light, and light as sound.

Similar experiments have been performed between the visual and tactile senses. If a baby is given a knobbly dummy/pacifier to suck (such that the baby has never seen this object but has only felt the shape in the mouth) and is then visually shown a smooth dummy/pacifier then what will happen? Will the baby recognize that the thing in the mouth has a different shape than the thing that is seen? Indeed it does. The baby looks at the dummy longer when there is a mismatch between touch and vision. The same is found if babies are allowed to explore objects in their hands without seeing them (e.g. a square and six-pointed star) and are then shown a star or square visually. They are able to match the tactile and visual sensations and they do so by picking out the shape that is new. This is partially related to Molyneux's question, discussed in Chapter 1 (namely whether a blind person, on seeing for the first time, will know shapes/objects by vision having known them previously by touch). In this instance, the infant has little experience of vision but *is* capable of matching touched shapes with seen shapes. It suggests a far greater mixing of knowledge between the senses than Locke would have believed. Their world may be blooming and buzzing, but it is not completely confused.

According to this intriguing theory, all of our separate senses (or partially separate senses) are carved out of a single, early unitary sense. How is this achieved? Some genetic influences are possible. That is, we are born pre-programmed to lose the ability to connect our senses. Or, at least, we lose it to the extent found in the newborn. There is some evidence for this. Studies of the brain anatomy in other species demonstrate that there are, early in life, direct connections between auditory and visual regions of the brain. These connections greatly diminish during the course of early development. However, our early day-to-day experiences also play a crucial role in determining the shape of our future senses. For example, infants possess the ability to hear all the subtly different sounds that make up the world's languages. As we develop we 'tune in' to our own language but, as a result, we effectively become deaf to sounds present in other languages. All the languages of the world are constructed out of a limited set of speech sounds, called phonemes. Some phonemes that are used in English are not used in other languages, and vice versa. For example, Japanese does not distinguish between 'r' and 'l'. However, Japanese infants can easily tell the difference between 'r' and 'l' and they would retain this ability if exposed to English or another suitable language at an early age. Japanese children and adults not previously exposed to 'r'/'l' languages have great difficulty in telling these sounds apart. They still hear the sounds, but they sound the same. Similarly, a red–green color-blind person still sees red and green as colored but the colors look the same (whatever that looks like). Their brains were born with a potential to experience red and green differently but the absence of a particular retinal cell puts paid to that.

Speech phonemes represent an example of how early experience may carve out a structure within a particular sense (hearing). But what about the links that exist between senses? Returning to the topic of blindness, discussed in Chapter 1, there is evidence that early blind people activate the visual parts of their brain in response to hearing and touch. This may reflect the retention of early intersensory pathways present in infants that are normally lost. An environmental trigger (damage to the eyes) may partially override the tendency for a separate visual sense to be carved away from our senses of touch and hearing. Thus, rather than thinking of blindness (or at least early acquired or congenital blindness) as being the absence of one sense, we could more controversially think of it as an amalgamated audiovisual and visuotactile sense that has no real counterpart in sighted people.

As I shall discuss at various points in this chapter, our perception of food is an example of multisensory processing *par excellence*. Food has taste, smell, tactile texture, temperature, color, and even sound (think of the crunch of a carrot). Moreover, our experience of food tells us that these sensory attributes tend to reliably co-occur. The taste of a strawberry is invariably accompanied by the smell of a strawberry, and the two are seldom parted. Some researchers have suggested that smell and taste fail to develop as fully segregated senses because of our interconnected experience of them, and other scientists such as Richard Stevenson even propose that smell–taste is a universal type of synesthesia found in everyone. We might describe a smell as 'sweet', but why? Sweet is a property of taste, not smell. We would not describe the smell of a dog as 'woof' or 'hairy'. Much of what we conveniently call 'taste' is an amalgam of smell and taste, and should properly be called flavor. As Stevenson states: 'Although no one has overtly claimed that flavor is a different sense to its principal components, smell and taste, this claim could certainly be argued' (i.e. a potential +1 to whatever count of the senses you are working with).

There is good evidence that smells derived from eating often tend to be treated as tastes rather than smells. Adding a sweet-smelling odor to a sweet-tasting liquid makes the liquid 'taste' sweeter, although a sweet odor will not make a salty liquid taste saltier. People who have lost their sense of taste (e.g. after a stroke) also lose the ability to categorize smells in terms of taste properties such as sweetness. This suggests that the use of taste adjectives to describe smells has a sensory basis rather than being rooted solely in language and metaphor. The links between taste and smell (i.e. our sense of flavor) are learned via our experiences with food, but the pathways in the brain that permit such learning are likely to be hardwired in the infant. Although vanilla smells sweet to a Westerner, it smells savoury to a Vietnamese. This is because vanilla tends to be accompanied by sucrose in Western cooking but not in the East. The smell of lemon is regarded as sweet in Vietnam (because lemon is frequently paired with sucrose) but sour in the West. An unfamiliar odor that is initially judged not to smell 'sweet', 'sour' or 'bitter' can acquire these labels very rapidly if paired with suitable tastes (e.g. sucrose, citric acid) and, once learned, is very robust to unlearning.

Having considered how synesthesia might occur in all infants and how multisensory combinations (e.g. flavor) are acquired and retained into adulthood via a mixture of hardwiring (i.e. genetics) and learning from experience, the next obvious question is how this relates to the types of synesthesia that we see in the small percentage of adults considered in Chapter 1. Perhaps some people retain the synesthesia of their infancy into adulthood, whereas the majority of people lose it or modify it? This claim has certainly been made by respected scientists such as Daphne Maurer and Simon Baron-Cohen. However, we only have to look at the types of synesthesia that are common in adults to realize that this claim can't be strictly true. Colored letters and numbers, or seeing the days of the week arranged in space around one's body, are particularly common types of adult synesthesia but we are certainly not born with knowledge of these concepts and nor are they acquired during infancy. I suggest, as an alternative account, that nobody retains their infantile synesthesia into adulthood. In contrast we all develop a mature system of linking our senses together and of linking our senses to non-sensory knowledge (e.g. knowledge of numbers). This development derives from these early trends and retains elements of it but is not, in any way, frozen in time. Moreover, different developmental trajectories can be taken depending on whether one possesses the synesthesia gene (present in the few) or not (the majority of people) or depending on whether one becomes blind (or similar) or not.

One of the first synesthetes that I had the pleasure of meeting was a man called James Wannerton. In 2001 there were still only a handful of researchers in the world interested in synesthesia and I was one of only a couple in the UK. In his email to me, he attached an Excel spreadsheet with a list of words and a description of what they tasted like to him. The list began as follows.

Absolute	'tangerines'
Academy	'chocolate bar, thin'
Accept	'egg yolk hard'
Acid	'acid drops'

Acquire	'condensed milk'
Acrobat	'chocolate biscuit, thick one'
Adams	'tomatoes, tinned'
Admit	'Smarties'
Adrian	'watery, incomplete'
Adventure	'vegetables, mashed?'

My initial reaction was a mixture of excitement and bafflement. I was excited because I had never come across anything like this before but I was baffled as to what might be going on. For those who experience colors for words, it is commonly found that words take on the color of the first letter. For example, all words beginning with 'A' are A-colored. It didn't take long to determine that James was different. One of the first things that I wanted to know was what this actually feels like. James replied saying that the sensations really do feel like tastes in his mouth. His descriptions have texture (watery or hard), temperature (cold bacon) as well as location (tongue, palette). His experiences probably involve some aspects of smell too (i.e. they are flavor descriptions), although we have tended to refer to them simply as 'taste' for convenience. The tastes automatically come to him when he is speaking, listening, thinking and even dreaming! A typical sentence would contain an ebb and flow of tastes over his tongue, some tastes being strong and others being weak or absent. Around half of the words in the dictionary have no taste at all, whereas others are strong enough to stop him in his tracks. For instance, the number 'six' has a very strong taste of vomit, but 'eight' doesn't have a taste at all. As with other types of synesthesia, his associations tend to be very consistent over time (more so than we would expect from his memory abilities). One of the most common questions I get asked about him is: is he fat or thin? Would all these tastes kill his appetite or make him constantly hungry? Although he can recount instances in which the taste of a word has spurred him to go and make a sausage sandwich, he is in fact tall and thin. The extent to which this is attributable to his synesthesia is unclear, but he certainly gets no calories from his synesthesia.

The reason I have introduced the example of James Wannerton at this point is that I believe it provides important clues as to how synesthesia might develop. James's sister also has synesthesia, suggesting a possible genetic component. However, his sister does not experience tastes; she experiences colors projected on to letters and words when reading. We do not know exactly why one synesthete develops the particular profile that they do. However, in James there was clear evidence of environmental influences that must have occurred, and they must have occurred much later than the infant-synesthesia phase. First of all, the more common a word is, the more likely it is to possess a synesthetic taste and the more intense the taste is rated. Secondly, the types of food that he experiences are not a representative sample of his present diet. In fact there are some things in his diet now that never appear in his synesthesia – beer, curries, garlic, for example. Conversely, there are plenty of foods in his synesthesia that he used to eat as a child but no longer does. Growing up in Britain in the 1960s was no culinary picnic, and James's synesthesia is littered with boiled vegetables, jam sandwiches and such-like. In fact, one third of the words that elicit a taste consist of various types of sweets, chocolate and cakes. James's synesthesia is based more around his childhood diet than his present one.

I showed James's descriptions to a colleague of mine, Julia Simner, who has a background in linguistics. She soon spotted that there were systematic trends in his synesthesia. For example, consider the words that, to James, elicit a taste of sausage sandwiches. These include 'knowledge', 'message', 'Stevenage' and 'village'. Note that these words have certain speech sounds in common – the 'idge' sound. The same was true of other tastes. There was an underlying logic and structure to his synesthesia, even though it did strike us as very bizarre. The sounds that tend to be important were also found in the names of the food themselves – e.g. the word 'sausage' also contains the 'idge' sound and elicits a taste of sausage (or sausage sandwich to be precise). Our explanation was that the learned associations between food names and their flavors provided the scaffolding upon which other synesthetic pairings between words and taste could be constructed. This construction would have been automatic and unintentional. (James would need a degree in linguistics to appreciate all the nuances of his system of synesthesia.) Once set up, the synesthesia may be very hard to unlearn in the same way as it is very hard to unlearn smell–taste pairings when they have been set-up. What is exceptional about James is that the experiences feel like taste sensations in his mouth, rather than learned memory associations. As we discovered in Chapter 1, this may depend on the extent to which the parts of the brain dedicated to perception (as opposed to memory) are activated. Just as color synesthetes may tend to activate color-selective regions of the brain, such as V4, James does the same with his taste-selective brain region, giving rise to his very real and concrete sensations.

For the remainder of this chapter, I'd like to turn away from the development of the senses to ask a different question. What are the advantages, if any, of processing the senses in a multisensory way rather than keeping each of our senses as separate and discrete? From a developmental perspective, one could imagine that the ultimate goal is to move away from the 'confusing' overlap of the senses that exists in the newborn. Are there any advantages to processing – say, flavor as a combined sense rather than as the sum of two parts? Or does it just reflect a meaningless by-product of the fact that different sensory experiences tend to reliably co-occur in our environments? I shall consider multisensory perception in general, rather than synesthesia in particular, because there is far more relevant evidence. In later chapters, I'll consider whether there are any particular advantages to having synesthesia (rather than the type of multisensory perception that we all have) and I'll consider the thorny issue of why synesthesia could have evolved as an alternative window onto the world. First of all I'll consider evidence from laboratory experiments and then I'll consider more 'real world' examples by returning to the topic of food perception.

When sound and vision collide

While most people will have come across visual illusions, illusions in other senses are less commonly known, and multisensory illusions in which several senses conspire in the deception are even less well known. However, multisensory illusions are everywhere – when you know how to look for them. The existence of these illusions offers important clues as to how the brain connects the senses together, and provides further evidence that our senses aren't as separate as we might think. It also provides the first clues as to why multisensory perception might be advantageous to an organism. Examples of some of these illusions can be found on the website that accompanies this book.

Imagine two bars moving along opposing trajectories on a computer screen, one from left to right and the other from right to left. This is illustrated in Figure 2. In the center of the screen the two bars briefly overlap. Following this, two bars can be seen again: one moving left to right, and the other moving right to left. But which bar is which? Does the bar moving left to right collide with the other bar and then return in a right-to-left direction? Or do the bars pass through each other, such that the left-to-right bar continues on its original trajectory? When presented with just this visual display, participants report that the bars pass on 96 percent of occasions and collide on only 4 percent. Psychologists even give a law to this: the law of good continuity. However, if a sound is played when the bars are near the center of the computer screen then a perceived collision becomes far more probable (39 percent of occasions). In this example, a sound is altering our perception of vision. Whether or not a collision is perceived depends crucially on the timing. If the sound is too early or late, the bars will be perceived as passing. Brain imaging studies show that the brain behaves differently on trials that are perceived to collide (suggesting that vision is altered by hearing) relative to those that are perceived to pass through each other (as is normally the case). This provides convincing evidence, if any were needed, that the way we perceive the world doesn't just depend on the information

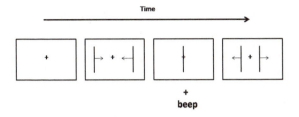

Figure 2 The two bars move together and then move apart. But do they collide or pass in the middle? A sound can alter the way that we perceive this visual event, changing our experience from passing to colliding.

relayed by our different sensory organs. It depends on how the brain integrates this information. The beep, by itself, does not signify a collision. The visual display, by itself, does not signify a collision. So if the senses of hearing and vision were always kept apart from each other then there would be no reason that we should ever perceive this as a collision. In this instance, two ambiguous events can be made meaningful if they are considered together, and the brain is always aiming to construct meaning out of ambiguity.

There is another multisensory illusion that more closely resembles synesthesia. In this illusion, called the 'double flash illusion', a beep doesn't just alter the direction of vision; it actually creates a visual experience that was never there. Imagine staring at the center of a computer screen. Suddenly you hear two beeps quickly in succession and, at the same time as the first beep, you are exposed to a brief flash in the periphery. What do you experience? On a proportion of these trials you will experience two flashes of light instead of one. It is as if the second beep has created a visual experience that was not there. When I say 'was not there' I mean, of course, not physically present in the environment (or in the eyes) but the second flash was physically present in the brain. We know this because electrical recordings from the visual part of the brain show that the illusory flash produces a similar effect in the brain as a real flash. As discussed before, activity in the visual parts of the brain may be all that is needed to create a visual experience. In some situations (as in this example) this could be elicited by a sound, even in someone who lacks synesthesia.

These two examples illustrate how the presence of a sound can affect the way we see the world. But can the reverse happen? Can the presence of misleading vision affect what we hear? There is an illusion called the 'McGurk illusion' that does just this. This illusion is based on the fact that when we listen to someone speaking we also extract visual information from their lip movements, provided the lips are in view. We are all quite proficient lip-readers even though we don't normally appreciate this fact. In the laboratory it is possible to edit movie clips of speech so that the visual lip movements say one thing and the heard speech says another. For example, the seen lips may be saying 'deal' and the heard speech is saying 'mail'. However, under these circumstances most people report hearing 'nail'. Close your eyes and the correct 'mail' sound is heard. Open your eyes again and you hear 'nail'. It is as if the visual information in the brain has combined with the auditory information to generate a perceptual experience that differs from that originally received by our sense organs – the 'n' sound was neither seen nor heard. However, it is not strictly correct to think of this illusion as an example of the brain making a mistake. In our everyday lives these conflicts rarely happen, except in badly dubbed movies. In most situations, lips and voices are perceived in harmony, and it is of considerable benefit for the brain to take advantage of this fact even if it does occasionally mislead.

In order to have a better understanding of these illusions we will need to dig deeper into the workings of the brain. The surface and the innards of our body contain a variety of different sensory receptors, as has already been mentioned. The function of these receptors is to translate physical signals (light, chemicals, pressure, and so on) into nerve impulses. Neurons are the basic type of cell that makes up all of our nervous system, including our brains. It is strange (but true) to think that a single type of cell is ultimately responsible for every facet of our mental life from feeling sad, playing music, reading a novel to walking and talking. Similarly, the whole range of sensory experiences must be explicable from the functioning of this single type of cell. If this is so, then how do we account for the diversity of sensory experiences, and why don't the signals become readily confused? The answer, according to the nineteenth-century neuroscientist Johannes Müller, was what he called the 'doctrine of specific nerve energies'. He assumed that each neuron was responsible for different types of information and each was associated with different sensations. Thus, a neuron carrying visual information would never carry auditory information, and a neuron carrying auditory information would never carry visual information. However, rules are made to be broken and the same applies to the doctrine of specific nerve energies.

Many neurons in the brain do, by and large, conform to the doctrine of specific nerve energies. For example, we have seen in Chapter 1 that neurons in the region of the brain called V4 are highly specialized for the processing of color. It is possible to have an experience of color by stimulating the neurons in V4 even if there are no colors to be seen. However, other neurons in the brain break with doctrine and appear to carry *both* auditory and visual information. These multisensory neurons combine sound and vision in ways that have important consequences for how we all perceive the world. For example, if one of these multisensory neurons is played a sound then it may produce ten nerve impulses. If it is shown a blob then it may produce 20 nerve impulses. However, if it is played a sound and shown a blob together it may produce 100 impulses. Thus the response is far greater than the sum of the parts. The multisensory neuron is acting like an internal amplifier that cranks up the volume of the sound and turns up the contrast on the image when the two co-occur. This is perhaps the main reason why multisensory perception is advantageous relative to fully segregated senses.

This internal amplification is very precise and occurs only under particular conditions. It tends to happen when the sound and the vision are simultaneous. This can explain why the two bars often appear to collide when a sound occurs at the critical time. The internal amplification is also greatest when the sound comes from the same point in space as the vision, and this can give rise to a different set of multisensory illusions. For example, when a ventriloquist moves the dummy's lips but suppresses his/her own lip movements the sound feels like it is coming from the dummy. The ventriloquist is *not* throwing his/her voice, as is commonly believed. Our brains expect sound and vision to come from the same location and we will adjust our perceptions accordingly. The illusion comes from our own ability in multisensory perception rather than the ability of the ventriloquist (whose ability lies solely in restricting his/her lip movements). In cinemas the speakers are primarily located at the sides of the auditorium, but we still perceive that the sounds come from the actors on the screen. There isn't a speaker behind the screen that follows the actor around. None is needed because our brains are geared to resolve ambiguities between vision and sound. This gives us a coherent picture of the world, even if the flip-side is a vulnerability to illusions.

When a large number of these multisensory neurons work together they can influence our behavior and give us certain advantages that would not be possible if our senses were strictly segregated. If one were to dilute a sweet solution with enough water, there would come a point at which the taster could not say for sure whether the solution was sweet, bitter or whatever. Similarly, one could reduce the concentration of an odor until it could no longer be identified by someone smelling it. The interesting question then becomes: can taste + smell combinations be identified in situations in which neither the smell nor taste can be reliably identified in isolation? The answer is yes. Pamela Dalton and colleagues gave participants a mixture of a sweet taste (saccharin) and a smell described as 'sweet' by most Westerners (a smell of almonds). Even though neither constituent could be identified in isolation, when they are combined the participants could detect the smell. As with the response properties of multisensory neurons, the whole is greater than the sum of the parts. Similar benefits have been reported in the audiovisual domain. Speech that cannot normally be heard because it is presented in a noisy room can become audible in the presence of watching somebody's lips. People often hear better when they put their glasses on.

There are plenty of other examples from other combinations of senses. Rather than go through each in detail, I will just list some of them below to give you a feel for what is known. In some instances, there is a clear benefit from integrating information from a secondary sense. In other instances, there is a distortion of perception as a result of information from a secondary sense – i.e. a multisensory illusion. I contend that illusions, although not always advantageous in themselves, can profitably reveal underlying mechanisms that are generally advantageous in most natural (i.e. non-laboratory) situations.

- Our hands are perceived as feeling dryer if we rub them together and the sound of the rubbing is amplified. The timing is crucial here. If the amplification is delayed by a fraction of a second then the illusion disappears.
- Similarly, an electric toothbrush feels smoother on the teeth when the sound level is reduced (even if the vibrations in the handset are constant).
- A picture feels like it is displayed longer and is judged to be brighter when it is accompanied by a sound, and sound is judged to be louder when accompanied by a bright visual stimulus.
- Our ability to detect whether we are touched on two points or a single point is improved if we can observe the part of the body touched – even if the object making the touch cannot be seen.
- Our balance (vestibular sense) can be affected if we are surrounded by a moving image. Fairgrounds often contain virtual 'rides' in which a standing (or sometimes seated) person is immersed in a projected visual movie of a roller-coaster or a plane flying over a cliff. The 'ride' itself never moves, but people have a strong sensation of tilt, movement, and vertigo.

This section has discussed how certain multisensory illusions can be created in the laboratory. These illusions demonstrate that the brain automatically integrates information from different senses and that it is normally advantageous to do so. A full segregation of the senses is not necessarily an optimal outcome of brain development. The issue of whether synesthesia in particular (rather than multisensory perception in general) carries any advantages will wait for a more detailed consideration later.

In the final section of this chapter, I shall venture outside of the laboratory in order to understand how multisensory perception affects our everyday lives, even though we are rarely aware of it. I shall return to a topic close to all our hearts – food.

From blind dinners to The Fat Duck

The restaurant Dans le Noir (literally meaning 'in the black') opened its doors to London diners in 2006, following the success of its sister restaurant in Paris. The restaurant serves food in pitch blackness so that the dining experience is not contaminated by visual expectations. As the man behind the London restaurant, Edouard de Broglie, explained to me: 'The preconception of what food tastes like because of what it looks like is gone. All your other senses are abruptly awoken and you will taste food like you have never tasted it before.'

Upon entering the restaurant I was given the key to a locker and asked to lock away bags, my mobile phone and even my watch, which the maître d' claimed might contain phosphorescent spots on the hours and hands.

'What's on the menu?' I asked.

'Every night is different' she replied unhelpfully. 'If you have special dietary requirements then we can take them into consideration, but you will not know what you are eating until you emerge afterwards.'

At this point, a waiter dressed all in black emerged from behind some thick red velvet curtains and asked me to place my right hand on his shoulder. He led me back behind the curtains and down a dark corridor. 'Hi, I'm Ash. If you need anything then just shout my name but don't attempt to move out of the chair without being guided by me.'

My initial uneasiness at having to touch my waiter had given way to the fear that he might leave me. Although we are all used to darkness there is something very unnerving about pitch black. In cities, we never properly experience it because of all the street lights. In the countryside, it is very rare because even the stars afford some light. As I sat down, I had no idea how big the restaurant was and my sense of space was shrunk to a bubble around me. I could hear a couple talking quite close to me on the left. They were debating whether the thing they were eating was fish or not!

My starter was a mixture of three different things. I had no idea what they were. The restaurant manager's words came back to me: 'You will taste food like you have never tasted it before' and I thought 'Well he's right, but the problem is that everything tastes so much blander in the dark.' I guessed, mainly on the basis of texture, that there was goat's cheese in the starter. However, when I subsequently saw the menu there was no goat's cheese on it. It may have been the liver (which I normally hate) or the seared tuna (which I thought might have been chicken) but it can't have been the grilled mushroom (I'd mistaken this for roasted pepper, as it had a slightly slimy texture). It also occurred to me that this must be the dilemma that James Wannerton is constantly facing. He knows that he has a certain taste and texture in his mouth, but what the hell is it? His synesthetic flavors cannot be seen any more than my meal could be seen.

When it comes to eating and drinking, our sense of vision does not contaminate or take anything away from our sense of flavor; it enhances it and is an integral part of it. The food industry and all the other sighted restaurants in the world have not got it wrong, and I'll consider some of the evidence below. Insofar as my sensory experience was enhanced by eating in the dark, it was limited to my sense of touch rather than taste or smell. Using a knife and fork in the dark is extremely difficult and I wondered how blind people do it. I thought that the cutlery would be like an extension of two fingers and that they would somehow be able to 'feel' the pressure, texture and location of the food on the end of the knife and fork in a way that was impossible to me. Having to resort to using my fingers (the main course was lamb stew and rice) was a surprising pleasure and it did enhance the culinary experience. It certainly made me more appreciative of the cultures where this is the norm.

At the other end of the restaurant experience, there is Heston Blumenthal's restaurant in the sleepy English village of Bray, The Fat Duck. His three-star Michelin restaurant was voted the best in the world in 2005. It is certainly innovative. His combinations of food have grabbed headlines with dishes such as snail porridge, and cauliflower risotto with chocolate jelly. These are not gimmicks but reflect a deep interest and knowledge in the science of food. In particular, he is interested in enhancing our appreciation of food by maximizing (rather than minimizing) the use of our other senses. Even the menu is for touching as much as seeing. It is printed on card that has a peculiar rubbery feel (not unlike the skin of a fat duck), and the touch somehow stays with you after you've put it down.

I had heard that Heston was interested in synesthesia, so I arranged to visit him to share ideas. When I arrived at the restaurant at 9 a.m., the chefs were already busy chopping and preparing. I had always assumed that science was very competitive, but it is nothing compared to top-end restaurants. I felt embarrassed that I had been unhappy about meeting so early (academics don't do anything at 9 a.m. unless they really must). As we talked he described how he tries to use other senses to create a perfect meal. For example, carrots can be made to 'taste' crunchier if the sound of the bite is recorded and amplified via headphones. He also serves a blood orange and beetroot jelly that plays on our color expectations. The juice of a blood orange is actually purple, and the juice of a yellow beet is orangey yellow. So the orange-flavored jelly looks like beetroot and the beet jelly looks like it should taste of orange. Most diners are fooled by the color unless they know in advance. I wondered whether a synesthete who tastes shapes, like Michael Watson, would be fooled by these jellies. Michael had lived in the USA and died many years ago. I knew of a synesthete, Linda, nearby who experienced visualized shapes when she tasted things. She gave the same synesthetic descriptions when she tasted the food with her eyes opened or closed. Linda's synesthesia may protect her from the normal illusion.

I told Heston about James Wannerton. Heston was particularly intrigued by James because he considers our experience of eating to be like the retrieval of a rich multisensory memory. James is effectively reliving previous meals whenever he hears or thinks about words.

'If he were eating strawberries and you were to say something that tasted of mint or cream, would these flavors combine?' Heston asked.

I had wondered about this before, but I had never actually asked James to try it out. Could you get a taste of strawberries and cream by combining real strawberries with synesthetic cream? I tried this out with James, using the word 'quiet' which tastes of condensed milk (the closest thing to cream that I could find in his synesthesia).

I get a lovely taste of strawberries and cream and it enhances the taste of the 'real' strawberries no end! 'Quiet' is a VERY strong tasting word so when I tried this the synesthetic taste did dominate over the strawberries, which weren't particularly strong. The taste induced by 'quiet' fades after a few seconds, a little like a fluorescent light does when you switch it off, but as soon as I articulate the word in inner speech then the dominance switches back from the actual food to the taste of the word.

I also tried getting him to say the words 'New York' (= runny egg yolks) while eating a piece of bread, and the real taste and synesthetic taste mixed here too.

I get the taste of thick, doughy bread and runny egg. The taste I get from bread and 'New York' is a lovely textural contrast. The combining of real and synesthetic experiences is one of the real pleasures I do get out of having synesthesia. For example, I love reading a newspaper and eating at the same time because I quite often come across pleasant combinations.

Eating toast and reading an article about New York would produce a very nice taste experience well beyond what I would normally get by merely eating a slice of toast.

I also wondered whether two synesthetic tastes could be mixed together. I got him to repeat, under his breath, pairs of words in succession such as 'husband, France, husband, France', etc. and 'princess, liberty, princess, liberty', etc. For James, 'husband' is honey and 'France' is wafers. The two words said together were nice and complemented each other, but he retained a sense of them being separate in his mouth. 'Princess' is runny mince and gravy while 'liberty' is yogurt. Unfortunately, these two liquidy tastes did mix and were described by James as horrible. It is perhaps unlikely to make it on to the menu at The Fat Duck.

We have undoubtedly become more health-conscious about our foods over the past 20 years, and the issue of food colorants has rightly or wrongly been at the center of this debate. Of course, not all food colorants are artificial and they are not all bad for you (whether artificial or not). Whatever we may think we want, our brains seem to want and expect our food to look a certain way. Some scientists have even suggested that monkeys and apes evolved color vision in order to enable them to distinguish between food-stuffs. The difference between a ripe tomato and an unripe one is primarily indicated by its color. Of course, ripe and unripe fruit also taste different, but we want an early defense mechanism that tells us this *before* we put something potentially unpleasant or harmful in our mouths. Color may serve that function.

In the early 1990s, the cola industry put two influential forces in competition with each other: our desire for things to be clear and pure versus our learned expectations about what food should look like. Our learned expectations won. Coca-Cola introduced 'TaB clear' and Pepsi-Cola introduced a brand called 'Crystal Pepsi'. Both products flopped and were pulled off the shelves after less than a year. The marketing logic behind them was that people would prefer to drink a clear alternative because clearness is equated with purity. The marketing tagline for Crystal Pepsi was 'you've never seen a taste like this'. However, people *had* seen a taste like this and it didn't taste of cola. A clear sparkling drink should, according to our expectations, taste of mineral water or lemonade; a dark brown drink should taste of cola. Perhaps even aside from our previous experience with cola, our brains are hardwired to expect strong-tasting drinks, such as cola, to have a strong coloration.

Even expert wine tasters can be thrown by the color. Wine experts will carry on using red-wine adjectives to describe the flavor of a white wine that has been adulterated with an odorless and tasteless red colorant. Other studies have shown that odors are more easily identified if they are appropriately colored. The intensity of an odor is rated as stronger if a solution is colored: the more saturated the color, the stronger is the effect. This can occur even if a color is inappropriate, so red-colored mint smells stronger than pink-colored mint.

Although color is the most obvious influence on flavor perception, touch and hearing are important too. Just as we have an expectation that stronger colored substances will have a stronger flavor, we tend to expect thicker substances to have less flavor. Thicker liquids are perceived as having weaker smells even if the amount of measured odor on the breath is physically the same. Sparkling water or champagne can be made to sound fizzier by amplifying the loudness or changing the pitch distribution (amplifying the higher pitched components). Pringles chips, cracked with the teeth, are judged to be crispier and fresher when the same auditory manipulations are used. In the 1980s Kellogg's even attempted to patent the specific cracking sound of its cornflakes.

In summary, multisensory perception is not some abstract concept that we can only study in the laboratory. It is a feature of virtually every product we buy and consume, and clever marketing is now making full use of our scientific knowledge of multisensory processing.

The first two chapters of this book have established a number of important principles that will contribute to an explanation of synesthesia. The first chapter established that sensory experiences, such as that of color, are a product of activity in specialized regions of the brain. In order to have an experience of color all we need to do is activate that part of the brain, and it matters little whether the input to the brain comes from seeing or hearing. The second chapter established that our senses are not as separate as we often assume, and that combining information from the senses is a key property of our brains, whether we have synesthesia or not. The next chapter will put these two pieces of the jigsaw together and will explain how the brain creates the altered reality that is synesthesia.

An altered reality

I consider synesthesia to be an altered reality. It is an alternative sensory window on to the world, and an alternative way of coloring our thoughts (or tasting them, etc.). In her first-hand account of having synesthesia, *Blue Cats and Chartreuse Kittens*, Pat Duffy puts it this way:

What each of us sees is the reality we know. I am at no more liberty to change the white color of the letter O than I am to change its circular shape; for me, the one is as much an attribute of the letter as the other.

Synesthesia bears an obvious resemblance to the types of multisensory perception and illusions described in Chapter 2, but we are not all, strictly speaking, synesthetes. It is tempting to conclude that we are all synesthetes to various degrees but, to me, that is more of a cop-out than an explanation. If one goes down this route, then one would still need to explain *why* some people are more of a synesthete than others, and *why* the über-synesthetes have the particular profile that they do. Why are letters colored and numbers arranged in space? Why not any other type of altered sensory experience that one could imagine? Explaining synesthesia is tricky because there are two opposing things that need to be accounted for. Synesthesia has similarities to normal multisensory perception, yet synesthesia is not the norm.

The account of synesthesia that I offer in this chapter aims to offer a coherent account of these two opposing facts.

I will explain how synesthesia is similar to the multisensory perception that we all engage in. The rules that we use to map between one sense and another appear to be common to synesthetes and non-synesthetes alike. For example, synesthetes tend to see high-pitched sounds as being smaller and lighter in color. People who lack synesthesia don't normally see anything when they hear a high-pitched sound but the same rules of association nevertheless operate at an unconscious level. I will also explain why synesthetes' perception is different. Why are their experiences conscious and why do they consist of the particular patterns that they do?

Crossing the Rubicon: from multisensory perception to synesthesia

The starting point for my explanation is that there are structured principles for dictating how the senses are linked. I mentioned this in the previous chapter and discussed how nature and nurture are both important. For example, infants can confuse sounds and lights if they are of the same intensity (nature) and taste–smell pairings can become fixed in the brain as a result of the way that they are combined in our culture's cooking (nurture). In this chapter, I will give several more examples and show how the same rules operate in synesthesia and normal perception. To get from normal multisensory perception (present in the many) to synesthesia (present in the few) involves adapting and reinforcing these rules. Something in the brains of synesthetes pushes them beyond a point of no return and into an altered reality of sensory experiences. What is it that is doing the pushing? As already discussed, synesthesia exists in several forms: a naturally occurring form with a genetic component, and acquired forms that arise after blindness (or other types of sensory less) or that arise temporarily after taking certain drugs. Each of these causes may manipulate the rules that govern multisensory perception in different ways, albeit giving a similar outcome – synesthesia.

It is to be noted that not all types of synesthesia are strictly 'multisensory'. Seeing letters and numbers evoking

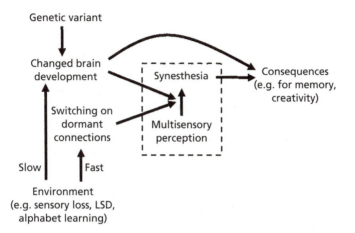

Figure 3 A model of synesthesia. The central part of the model explains synesthesia in terms of adaptations to normal mechanisms of multisensory perception. The adaptations themselves reflect either altered brain development or switching on of dormant connections (the left-hand side of the model), which are themselves a product of genetic and/or environmental influences. The right-hand side of the model considers other potential consequences of having synesthesia (e.g. are synesthetes more creative?) and two possible scenarios: the consequences of synesthesia are related directly to the altered sensory experiences (shorter straight arrow), or the consequences of having synesthesia are due to the structural changes in the brain irrespective of the precise sensory experiences (longer curved arrow).

color is visual–visual. However, different aspects of vision are implicated (shape and color) and the same basic principles of how different things get connected apply just as well in this example. Even with colored letters and numbers, there is often a true multisensory component to it. Speech or touched letters often elicit the same colors as letters seen visually and yet another sense, proprioception, can contribute to the perceived spatial location of the color.

Figure 3 schematically outlines the model that I will unpack in this chapter. The model has three basic parts. The central part of the model states that synesthesia is effectively an adaptation of the normal processes of multisensory perception that is universal among humans and many other species (although we can't be certain whether other species have synesthesia, we can be certain that they have multi-sensory perception). The left-hand part of the model accounts for the various causes of synesthesia and the effects that they have on the brain. The naturally occurring form of synesthesia has a genetic component that alters the pattern of wiring in the brain. In these synesthetes, different regions of the brain that are close to each other may tend to stay connected as the brain matures. This may explain why some types of synesthesia are more common than others and why certain things seem to go together in synesthesia. For example, synesthetic colors seem to depend on the spellings of words but synesthetic tastes depend on the sounds of words. This could be explained by the way that different brain regions get wired together. Genes are not the whole answer, because many of the things that trigger synesthesia (e.g. letters, numbers) are culturally learned and some of the experiences are too (e.g. the taste of sausage sandwiches). Acquired types of synesthesia are assumed to be caused solely by events in the environment such as being unfortunate enough to damage one's eyes, being blindfolded for several days, or taking a mind-altering substance. The effects on the brain are not fully understood but it is possible that there are two different mechanisms, one slow-acting and one fast-acting. Sometimes synesthesia appears after a few hours or days (e.g. after taking LSD and in some cases of blindness) and at other times it appears to take months or years (in some cases of blindness). There could be hidden connections in the brain that permit synesthesia if they are switched on, although normally they lie dormant. In other cases, a slower reorganization of multisensory pathways in the brain is likely, involving the creation of new connections.

Finally, the third part of the model on the right-hand side concerns the consequences of having synesthesia. Does having synesthesia make you more artistic, give you a better memory, or give you difficulties in reading? I make a distinction between two types of consequences of having synesthesia. As you will have gathered, there are many different types of synesthesia and this makes it difficult to

determine whether any consequences are due to one particular type of synesthesia (such as colored music) or to
synesthesia in general. For example, it is widely claimed
that synesthetes are more likely to be artistic. But is this
true of particular types of synesthetes (e.g. those experiencing visual synesthesia) or all types of synesthetes? Would
people who feel shapes in their hands when they taste or
people who experience tastes when they see words be more
artistic? Possibly not. In the model, I make this distinction
by considering whether the consequences of synesthesia are
linked to the underlying brain changes (the curved arrow at
the top of Figure 3) or to the particular sensory symptoms
of the synesthesia (the smaller arrow at top right). The
consequences of having synesthesia will be considered more
carefully in subsequent chapters, but other aspects of the
model are considered here.

One of the most common types of synesthesia is colored
letters and numbers. Why? The idea that this reflects expo-
sure to colored alphabet books has largely been discounted.
The colors of synesthetes are often very peculiar: dirty
colors, transparent colors, or strange mixes of two colors. In
contrast, colored alphabet books are invariably in primary
colors. Attempts to link individual synesthetes' colors with
published alphabet books have been largely unsuccessful.
One suggestion made by V.S. Ramachadran in San Diego
is that letters and numbers are colored because the part
of the brain that recognizes them is next to the part of
the brain that enables experiences of color (area V4 that
was encountered in Chapter 1). In synesthesia, an altered
genetic profile may result in parts of the brain being
strongly connected that would only be weakly connected in
other people. Moreover, there may be a natural tendency for
this altered connectivity to affect nearby regions rather
than long-distance as this is a general principle of how
brains are wired. This has been termed the adjacency principle. The hypothetical synesthesia gene may tend to promote connectivity between brain regions that are adjacent
to each other.

Other types of synesthesia can be explained by this
principle. A different part of the brain to that used to

recognize letters and numbers is used to process the spatial relationship between objects. Space is a very important aspect of most, if not all, types of synesthesia and the next chapter is dedicated to it. The most common types of synesthesia involve space and consist of seeing ordered sequences such as days, months, letters, and numbers arranged in space – gliding through the mind's eye or encircling the body. The part of the brain used to represent word sequences lies next to the part of the brain that codes space and the synesthesia gene may reinforce connections between these regions. One of the synesthetes that I have encountered also associates colors with sequences such that the first items of a sequence (e.g. 1, Monday, January) have the same color, as do the second items (e.g. 2, Tuesday, February), and so on.

For other synesthetes, it isn't the position in the sequence, but rather the meaning, that determines the color. This can be conveniently illustrated with numbers, because numbers can be denoted in many ways but retain the same meaning. For instance, the number 5 can be expressed as a digit (= 5), as a word (FIVE), as counting on five fingers, or as five dots (e.g. a dice pattern). One of the synesthetes that we studied, called Tim, reported a remarkable form of synesthesia involving numbers. He states that not only are digits colored but dice patterns are colored too, and his hands become colored when he counts on them! He counts in a particular way, starting with his thumb outstretched on his left hand and then uncurling the index, middle, ring and little fingers before moving on to the right hand. The exposed part of his palm and the outstretched fingers (but not the curled fingers) appear colored to him, and as each finger is uncurled the hand flips in color to reflect the new number created. The colors themselves are determined by the meaning of the number (i.e. the amount). Thus, 5 is a brownish cardboard-box color irrespective of whether it is seen as a written digit, as a dice pattern, or as five outstretched fingers. The regions of the brain that deal with the order and amount denoted by numbers are different from those used to recognize the physical form of numbers (e.g. the shape of the written digit) and different synesthetes may use these different regions, presumably depending on where in the brain the gene is expressed.

My main input into this theory was based on our observations of synesthetes who experience tastes from words, such as James Wannerton. When I first met James it was quite obvious that his synesthesia was operating on different principles than in those who experience colored letters. For letter–color synesthetes, words tend to be colored by dominant letters in the word such as the first letter. For example, words beginning with A would tend to all have the color of the letter A. However, the taste of James's words had nothing to do with the tastes he experienced for letters. Instead, similar sounding words tended to have the same taste, and the words tended to evoke tastes with similar sounding names. Thus, 'Barbara' tastes of rhubarb, 'Virginia' tastes of vinegar and 'auction' tastes of Yorkshire pudding. For people with colored letters, 'glue' tends not to be blue and 'mellow' tends not to be 'yellow'. However, having studied only one person with this type of synesthesia we couldn't be sure whether it was a general feature of James's type of synesthesia or a peculiar characteristic of James! We got to know about many more cases of this type of synesthesia from both North America and Europe; they all showed the same pattern as James and they were all very different from the letter–color synesthetes. So James wasn't unusual. The taste of words is triggered by completely different things than the color of words. Their tastes were all influenced by the sounds of words rather their spellings. For example, there was a bizarre tendency for 'Friday' to taste of something that is fried! The taste of 'Friday' for seven of these synesthetes is listed below.

Jennifer – 'thick french fries'
James – 'fried spam'
Deborah – 'fried egg whites'
Suzanne – 'sweet batter'
Lucy – 'something deep-fried in batter, greasy'
Michelle – 'macaroni sauce'
Christine – 'no taste'

The parts of the brain dedicated to taste and flavor perception are far away from those dedicated to color perception and letter recognition, but are close to regions involved in the processing of spoken language. As such, we proposed that localized differences in the way that the brain is connected can account for these two very different patterns of synesthesia. These connections are presumably present very early in life, but they mature as the brain acquires knowledge of food and words. Letters tend to go with colors, and spoken language tends to go with taste as a result of the coincidental locations of these sensory centers within the brain.

Depending on where in the brain the gene tends to get expressed, potentially different types of synesthesia will result. Given that synesthetes often have multiple types of synesthesia, it is likely that the gene exerts fairly widespread influences in the brain. In principle, there is no reason why these differences in the brain should occur only for regions involved in creating sensory experiences. Some have argued that as well as giving rise to synesthetic experiences, these changes in the brain may give synesthetes other strengths and weaknesses. This will be returned to in the final chapter. It may also give rise to unusual non-sensory associations in synesthetes. One curious thing that seems to go hand in hand with synesthesia is a tendency to attribute genders and personalities to things such as letters or numbers. For example, one synesthete noted that '1, 2, 3 are children who play together. 4 is a good peaceful woman, absorbed by down-to-earth occupations . . . 5 is a young man, ordinary and common in his tastes and appearance.' Another person described 3 as 'male; definitely male. Three is such a jerk! He only thinks of himself. Five is a king.' Viewing displays of random letters and numbers during an experiment was described as like viewing people at a dinner party! I would not class this as a type of synesthesia in its own right because the experience isn't a sensory one. Nonetheless, it could well be a by-product of more widespread differences that exist in the brains of people who have synesthesia and hence it resembles synesthesia in all other important respects.

In the model that I outlined above, the naturally occurring forms of synesthesia are assumed to reflect a contribution of environmental factors as well as genetic ones. For instance, letters are culturally learned. Some people acquire Chinese letters, others the English alphabet, and many people in the world remain illiterate. We know little about what synesthesia is like prior to learning to read or in illiterate cultures although it is reasonable to assume that synesthesia would still exist in some shape or form. Pat Duffy recalls that prior to learning to read and write each word had its own colorful 'design' that she used to love to draw. These designs eventually gave way to colored letters as she learned to say the alphabet and copy letters down, but she is unsure how the colors of her letters are related to her preliterate designs that are now forgotten.

All the alphabet letters that I learned had color right away . . . For some reason, it took me a very long time to draw the letter R. I tried again and again, but just couldn't get the hang of it . . . Then one day, staring a long time at R, I noticed how similar in form it was to P. The only difference between the two letters was that a slanted line came down from P's head. This meant that if I could make a P, I *could* make an R! . . . And unlike the light yellow of P, its color was orange. I marvelled that a yellow letter could become an orange letter just by drawing a line!

Pat works as a translator for the United Nations in New York and as an adult she attempted to learn Chinese. Chinese tends to be taught initially using the English alphabet in a system called Pinyin. After the speaker is more proficient, the Chinese characters are introduced. Pat was able to use her existing synesthesia based on the Pinyin in order to learn the new characters.

Carol Mills of Goucher College has reported the case of a polyglot who speaks English, Russian, Spanish, French, Polish, German and Old Church Slavic. All of her second languages were acquired in adulthood. Russian, which uses a different alphabet, took on the colors of the English alphabet such that similar-shaped letters have the same colors. This includes the mirror-reversed letters that appear in Russian. Those letters that don't have a similar shape to English letters took on the color of the sound. Learning Polish was hard for her because it has many of the same sounds as Russian but is written in the English alphabet.

Language has always been for me very real stuff. It's not just the sort of transparent something that you speak through. It's always been imageable . . . Russian very quickly seemed to just make its own parasitic color code off of our alphabet. So for instance, if you take the Russian letter that sounds like V but looks like B, it's the same shape as a B so it has the same color as English B which is very intense black. But it's not the same texture; it has metallic things on it.

I have studied several letter–color synesthetes who have learned to read music fluently. In English, musical notes are named after the letters A to G and the synesthesia migrated across to musical notes based on the established colors of letters. Thus, all A-notes would be the color of the letter A irrespective of how the note was written (minim, crotchet, quaver, etc.) or the clef it was written in (bass or treble). George Sachs, the colorful albino of Chapter 1, was noted to have this too. Letters are used to label musical notes in his native language of German. Of course, it is purely a cultural quirk that we happen to use letters in that way but synesthesia isn't choosy about that. As a more extreme example, it is perhaps little more than a cultural quirk that we read with our eyes rather than our finger tips. We could, in principle, do the latter (the blind do it, after all). If we did then I suspect that touch–color synesthesia would go from being one of the rarest types of synesthesia to being one of the most common, although it would effectively be just another example of letter–color synesthesia (based on touched rather than seen letters). The part of the brain that recognizes printed letters can also recognize touched letters such as in Braille, so a similar brain mechanism would produce a completely different outward manifestation according to ones culture.

Acquired types of synesthesia have different characteristics to the naturally occurring forms. They tend not to be based on cultural symbols such as letters, numbers and words. Instead non-linguistic sounds may trigger vision, or touch may trigger a flash of light. This may be partly because the onset of acquired synesthesia occurs after this basic knowledge has been learned, whereas in the naturally occurring forms the brain is wired differently from day one such that when this knowledge is acquired it instantly becomes imbued with color, taste and other sensations. The acquired types of synesthesia are assumed to have a purely environmental trigger. In acquired synesthesia, the brain would initially be wired the same as everyone else but would reorganize itself or switch on a dormant pathway following a trigger. In naturally occurring synesthesia, the synesthesia gene could be viewed as tending to create novel types of multisensory perception (e.g. colored letters) whereas non-genetic, acquired variants of synesthesia would tend to be based more on the multisensory processes found in non-synesthetes. This division is by no means absolute, as several types of naturally occurring synesthesia have close parallels with non-synesthetic multisensory perception. This includes visual experiences from music (discussed later) and experiencing touch when somebody else is observed being touched (discussed in Chapter 5).

Synesthesia that arises after blindness (or other forms of sensory loss) is known to occur, although it has not been extensively documented and it is unclear how common it is. It is assumed to reflect a kind of internal compensation such that when the visual parts of the brain fail to receive input from vision then other pathways into the visual region become strengthened. These include pre-existing connections from the other senses. It is like switching the lights on from the inside out, rather than the outside in. Sometimes this can occur quickly, after a day or two. Sighted individuals who are completely blindfolded for a couple of days also report visual experiences. This fast timescale suggests that pathways linking the senses in the brain that are normally dormant become used. However, the time it takes for synesthesia to emerge appears to be very variable, with some reporting that it takes months or years. This suggests a different mechanism involving creating new connections in the brain. In the model that I have outlined, this is illustrated by slow and fast routes from environmental inputs.

The effects of hallucinogenic drugs in creating altered sensory experiences are not well understood despite the research programs that were conducted in the 1950s and 1960s, including by the CIA, who wanted to use these drugs as a kind of truth serum. The reports of a generation of people who tried these substances attests to their 'miraculous' properties, as do reports of intentional and accidental use throughout the ages. The use of these substances in religious sacraments has been found in almost every ancient tradition. The hallucinatory experiences were typically regarded as giving insight into another world, or dreamlike prophecies of this world. The use of musical sounds and incantations may have promoted the synesthetic dimension of these substances. The Aztecs used the peyote cactus; the Australian Aborigines chewed pituri, a desert shrub; the natives of the upper Amazon had yagé vine. The ergot fungus, from which LSD is derived, grows on rye and is likely to have been central to the oldest religion in the west, called the Eleusinian mysteries, whereby for two millennia pilgrims would come once a year to drink the holy brew (including greats like Plato and Aristotle). In Europe, the medieval chronicles describe how bread would sometimes be infected with ergot and whole villages would go 'mad' for a few days. This came to be known as Saint Anthony's fire and it was no medieval Summer of Love. In large doses ergot is poisonous and the hallucinatory, and presumably synesthetic, experiences would be viewed with extreme fear by the pious and unwitting population.

The research of the 1950s and 1960s was concerned with documenting the easily measurable outcomes of these drugs – heart rate, visual ability, and so on. As such the inner experiences were of secondary importance and synesthesia, which cannot be externally observed, was never a central feature of the research. However, the synesthetic and hallucinatory experiences were very much a central part of the first-hand accounts of people who had taken the drugs. The following is an abbreviated account of a self-experiment by the psychiatrist Werner Stoll, who in 1947 was the first person to publish an account of the effects of LSD in a scientific journal.

At 8 o'clock I took 0.06 mg of LSD. Some 20 minutes later, the first symptoms appeared: heaviness in the limbs . . . a certain euphoria then set in . . . and I went 'sailing' around the room with large strides . . . there followed an unprecedented experience of unimaginable intensity that kept increasing in strength. It was characterized by an unbelievable profusion of optical hallucinations that appeared and vanished with great speed, to make way for countless new images. I saw a profusion of circles, vortices, sparks, showers, crosses, and spirals in constant, racing flux . . . All were colored: bright, luminous red, yellow, and green predominated . . . I had to force myself to give a description. Terms like 'fireworks' or 'kaleidoscopic' were poor and inadequate . . . Often I had peculiar bodily sensations: I believed my hands were attached to some distant body, but was not certain whether it was my own. As I washed them, it was happening a long way from me, somewhere down below on the right. It was questionable, but utterly unimportant, whether they were my own hands . . . I observed that random noises, and also noises intentionally produced by the supervisor of the experiment, provoked simultaneous changes in the optical impressions (synesthesia). In the same manner, pressure on the eyeball produced alterations of visual perceptions . . . On the way home and in the evening I was again euphoric, brimming with the experiences of the morning. I had experienced unexpected, impressive things. It seemed that a great epoch of my life had been crowded into a few hours.

These drugs offer a unique window into another reality that has inspired writers, musicians and artists. As the discoverer of LSD who worked under Werner Stoll, Albert Hofmann, noted:

Of greatest significance to me has been the insight that what one commonly takes as 'the reality' by no means signifies something fixed, but rather something that is ambiguous – that there is not only one, but that there are many realities.

I do not wish to draw too strong a parallel between the drug-induced psychedelic state and the day-to-day experiences of people born with naturally occurring forms of synesthesia. However, it would be surprising if there were no similarities between them. As with the types of synesthesia found in blindness, those observed in psychedelic states tend not to involve learned symbols such as letters, numbers and words and are more likely to reflect phenomena such as visualized music. Rather than creating new types of multisensory combinations, drug-induced synesthesia may be utilizing the normal mechanisms that link our senses. They bring dormant connections to the fore. In the model above, drugs such as LSD work almost exclusively on the fast route with very little evidence of long-term changes to sensation after taking the drug (except in a few habitual users). Perhaps surprisingly, given the vivid visual experiences, the visual abilities of people inebriated with these drugs deteriorate rather than improve while under the influence. For instance, they find it harder to tell similar colors apart even though their sensations of color feel more intense rather than washed out. As with blindness, the switching on of the visual parts of the brain from the inside out (e.g. from the other senses) may go hand in hand with reducing the input from the outside in.

The same is certainly not the case in the naturally occurring types of synesthesia. These synesthetes have been shown to have significantly better abilities in perceiving color. When given color chips of equal brightness which they have to sort into order, for instance to make a color series from yellow to green, people who experience synesthetic colors perform better than controls who lack synesthesia. This is intriguing. Acquired types of synesthesia seem to be due to sensory deprivation (perhaps including the drug-induced forms), but naturally occurring synesthesia seems to be associated with better perceptual abilities. One possibility is that normal multisensory perception exists in a sort of balanced equilibrium in terms of the way information is transmitted between different aspects of perception. Synesthesia destroys that balance in terms of either sensory flooding (leading to enhanced perception) or sensory deprivation (associated with worse perception), but both lead to one brain mechanism driving another sensory process.

Why 'O' is white and Chopin is yellow

All synesthetes at some point in their life wonder why particular things evoke the specific sensations that they do. Why is my A red? Why is this note on the flute a golden streak? Why is my number 1 over there? Until quite recently, many researchers of synesthesia believed that this was a fruitless line of questioning, given that every person has their own idiosyncratic choice of colors, and not even family members can agree on what the 'correct' colors are. But this is only half true. For any given individual, it is virtually impossible to be certain why any particular thing elicits the sensation that it does. But if one looks at a sufficient number of different synesthetes, a more interesting picture emerges. Consider the letters of the alphabet. Forty-three percent of synesthetes think that A is red, 58 percent think that B is blue or brown, 29 percent think that C is yellow, and 49 percent think that the letter O is white. These fall far short of 100 percent agreement amongst synesthetes, but they are also far higher than one would expect from a purely random association of letters with colors. In English, we tend to categorize colors into 11 basic labels (black, white, red, blue, green, yellow, brown, orange, gray, purple, and pink) which gives a baseline probability of 9 percent, all things being equal.

Even more intriguingly, people who lack synesthesia show some evidence of the same trends. If you ask people what color the letter A is, they will say 'what are you talking about?' If you force them to choose a color, any color, then about 40 percent of them choose red. They have no real commitment to their answer and may easily change it to another color if asked again (although still around 40 percent of people will pick red). This differs from true synesthesia in which the colors remain resolutely fixed over time. In the central part of my model outlined above I suggest that the rules of association that apply in synesthesia can also be found in the multisensory processes of the general population. One of the key lines of evidence for this assertion comes from the similarities between the 'real' sensory experiences of synesthetes and the (normally unconscious) multisensory associations that lurk within our own minds. In this section, I will consider color associations with sounds, letters, numbers, and other ordered sequences. I have already considered how words come to acquire tastes and noted that similar principles operate over different synesthetes (e.g. the taste of Friday). In Chapter 4, I'll also discuss the spatial relationships that exist in many types of synesthesia. Almost all of this research has come from the naturally occurring form of synesthesia.

Those synesthetes who experience vision from music and other sounds come closest to the psychedelic world discussed above. Their experiences consist of a wildly fluctuating flow of colors, shapes, textures, and movement that dance in time with the music; sometimes in a three-dimensional mist that comes towards them like walking through rain. It is perhaps not surprising that many of these synesthetes develop an interest and aptitude in both music and the visual arts. Rolf, a professional illustrator, describes the following.

Synesthesia changes something that drifts through the air and into the ear into an almost tangible experience. I can sort of 'bathe' in the music like a concert-goer does, only at home, and the effect never diminishes. I enjoy many varied types of music. I always hear John Lennon's voice as something like red cellophane (the type you get around toffee apples) – it has to be red. A CD of piano music can give a very good synesthetic response. I like the way the piano goes from dark brown to bright yellow as the notes get higher. A quick succession of high notes appears almost like a moving star cluster, and an arpeggio like a printed pattern spooling in front of my eyes. It can be very sensual, I suppose related to ballet or dance (though I have a poor sense of rhythm and coordination) – an animated spectacle.

With such complex experiences, one might imagine that it is impossible to explain why they appear the way that they do. It is true that the science can do little justice to the obvious beauty of the visions, but it is wrong to assume that science can make no inroads at all. One explanation can be discounted straight away, namely that there is a lawful relationship between the frequency of the sound waves and the frequency of the electromagnetic spectrum that can give rise to sensations of color. The descending musical pitches do not trigger color experiences in the descending order of wavelengths – red, orange, yellow, green, blue, indigo and violet. In the eighteenth century, several musicians developed color organs that projected color when certain notes were played and the notes were typically arranged according to Newton's spectrum of colors, which had first been reported in 1672. These organs almost certainly had nothing to do with synesthesia, because synesthetes do not show such an arrangement of color with sound.

In 1975, Larry Marks reviewed many historical reports of this type of synesthesia and concluded that there was a meaningful relationship between the pitch of a musical note and the lightness and brightness of the synesthetic visions. High-pitched notes tended to be lighter and brighter, whereas low-pitched notes tended to be darker and dimmer. There is anecdotal evidence to suggest that the same trend is found in synesthesia induced by hallucinogens. I have recently shown the same trend in a group of present-day naturally occurring synesthetes and directly compared them to control participants who lack synesthesia. Given that the controls did not have any visual experiences, they were asked to choose the 'best' color to go with the sound. Whereas synesthetes tended to choose very similar colors if given the same sound twice, the controls were more variable. Nevertheless, in other respects there was a striking similarity between them. Both controls and synesthetes showed a relationship between ascending pitch and the increasing lightness of the color. This occurred for different types of instrument (e.g. piano and string instruments) and was comparable for synesthetes and controls. This suggests that everyone has access to the same underlying rule of multisensory association even if it is accessed in different ways: synesthetes literally see it in their visual experiences to music but people who lack synesthesia must infer it.

For those who lack synesthesia, the multisensory rule that links auditory pitch and visual lightness is probably inferred automatically rather than relying on slow, deliberate reasoning. Another study by Larry Marks presented non-synesthetes with sounds and asked them to judge whether each was high or low in pitch. At the same time, they were shown shaded gray patches on the screen that were irrelevant to the task. On some occasions a high-pitched tone may be paired with a lighter gray; on other occasions it may be paired with a darker gray. People were significantly faster at determining whether a pitch is high or low when the high pitch is coincidentally paired with light gray and the low pitch is paired with dark gray than vice versa. The same results are found if participants are asked to decide whether the gray is light or dark and ignore whether the auditory pitch is high or low. Similar findings are found when words are used instead of actual sensory experiences. A sneeze is thought of as bright, whereas a cough is dark. Sunlight is loud and moonlight is quiet. These meaningful associations are frequently used in literature and poetry. Edgar Allan Poe spoke of 'the murmur of the gray twilight'. Rudyard Kipling noted that 'the dawn came up like thunder' and Percy Shelley described a 'soft yet glowing light, like lulled music'.

Toddlers show evidence of the same rule. Cathy Mondloch and Daphne Maurer showed toddlers two bouncing balls – one black and one white. They were played a sound such as a high-pitched squeak or a low-pitched thud and were asked which ball was making it. The toddlers tended to match the squeak with the white ball. Of course in real life white balls don't make higher pitched sounds. This suggests that the rule is not learned from direct observation. Even one-month-old infants can match auditory pitch with visual brightness.

The other rule that is found early in life and appears to be very reliable in synesthetes and non-synesthetes alike is a tendency to associate pitch with vertical position in space. Thus, high-pitched sounds are literally seen by synesthetes as high in space and low-pitched sounds are literally seen by synesthetes as low in space. This may seem very obvious, but it isn't. Why are high-pitched sounds high? Why use a spatial metaphor for a non-spatial aspect of a sound? Of course, the effect could be driven by language itself. Synesthetes see high pitch as high because our language happens to use spatial words for describing pitch. A more interesting alternative is that our choice of language is driven by a basic multisensory rule, i.e. that we use spatial words for describing pitch because there is an underlying sensory association between pitch and space. This is almost certainly the case, because infants who have yet to learn language look at an up arrow (↑) when shown an 'ascending' pitch and at a down arrow (↓) with 'descending' pitch. It is probably no coincidence that our system of musical notation also tends to represent pitch in terms of vertical position on the stave. In doing so, this purely cultural invention dovetails perfectly with our brains' natural expectations about pitch and space.

There is a systematic relationship between pitch and size. Thus, not only are high-pitched sounds lighter in color and higher in space than low-pitched sounds, but they are also smaller in size. A similar trend is found in people who lack synesthesia. Again, people are faster at judging the pitch of a sound if high pitch is accompanied by an irrelevant small visual object and low pitch is accompanied by a large one. In this instance, the rule could possibly be derived from experience. Large objects (e.g. an elephant) do tend to make lower pitched sounds than small objects (e.g. a mouse). Synesthesia is not picky about this. It can latch on to whatever structure exists in the brain, irrespective of whether the structure was put in place via experience or via hard-wiring.

Music consists of far more than a series of different pitches. The rhythm, dynamics, melody and harmony can all influence the synesthesia and contribute to the rich and ephemeral quality of the visual experiences. Their effects on synesthesia are harder to study and are not well documented.

Most synesthetes to whom I have spoken, do not experience each note of the music in isolation. The notes merge together into an elaborate chain to which new links are added all the time and the old links trail off in to the distance to some vanishing point. Musical notes that are longer in duration tend to be longer in visual length, i.e. a synesthetic association between time (in our sense of hearing) and space (in vision). A continuously bowed note on the violin would tend to be seen as long but a plucked note would be small and round.

Just as there is a lawful relationship between visual lightness and auditory pitch, a comparable relationship exists between lightness and number. Numbers are frequently reported to elicit color in synesthesia, and the lower the number, the lighter is the color. Zero, 0, is often described as clear or transparent and 1 is often white. Number 9 is often dark. After 10, the pattern normally breaks down because a number such as 10 comprises two digits, each with its own color, and it is very rare for multi-digit numbers to have their own color. In non-synesthetes, the same trend is found. Participants presented with pairs of digits (e.g. 2 and 7) are faster at deciding which is numerically larger when 2 is light and 7 is dark than if 2 is dark and 7 is light. The same result is found if participants are asked to decide which of the digits is printed in a lighter color. They are faster at saying that 2 is light and 9 is dark than at saying that 2 is dark and 9 is light.

One might imagine that other concepts that can be ordered (such as letters of the alphabet, days of the week, and months of the year) would also show a relationship between the lightness of the synesthetic color and the order in the sequence. Although I am not aware of this ever being directly tested, the evidence available suggests not. Other principles seem to be involved. The situation with colored letters is complex, as several factors are implicated. Before I explain our results, have a go at a quick test: generate as many colors as you can in 30 seconds. Go. There is no right or wrong answer to this test, but people tend to behave systematically rather than randomly. The most common order in which colors come to mind is: yellow, blue, green, red, black, white, purple, orange, brown, pink, and gray. The first items to be generated are the most prototypical colors. But they are not the most common color words in the English language, which are 'black', 'white', and 'red'. When we asked our control participants to associate colors with letters of the alphabet they showed evidence of using this strategy. However, our synesthetes did not. They did something far more interesting.

In 1969 two linguists, Brent Berlin and Paul Kay, conducted a survey of how different languages of the world assign names to colors. Perhaps surprisingly, there are strong cultural differences over how colors are named and how many basic color terms there are. In English, they identified 11 basic color terms which were listed above. Other cultures can have as few as two. They found that there is an order in which new colors tend to be added to the vocabulary of any given language. This order is listed below. Thus, a language with only two color words, found in some parts of New Guinea, would tend to divide the colors into light and dark. This would correspond to black and white in English, with other dark colors (such as brown and blue) being called 'black' and other light colors (such as red and yellow) lumped together under the label 'white'. A language with three color words, such as Ejagam (spoken in Nigeria and Cameroon) and Wobé (Ivory Coast) would tend to have red as the third color category. A language with four or five color words, such as Iduna (spoken in New Guinea) and Cayapa (spoken in Ecuador), would introduce green and/or yellow. And so on.

1 Black, white
2 Red
3 Green, yellow
4 Blue
5 Brown
6 Orange, purple, gray, pink

The origins of this ordering remain controversial although Berlin and Kay claim that it reflects the biological structure of our sense of vision. Another possibility is that it reflects the frequency with which colors can be found in naturalistic environments, with colors at the bottom of the hierarchy being relatively rare. Whatever the origin, synesthetes link more common letters of the alphabet with the first colors in this hierarchy and the less common letters of the alphabet with later colors in the hierarchy. Thus, common letters such as E, T, A, O, and I tend to have common colors such as black, white, red, green, yellow, and blue. Rare letters such as K, X, J, Q, Z tend to have rarer colors such as purple, pink, orange, and gray. The same pattern was not found in our control participants. Our results suggest that synesthetes have linked together letters and colors in a systematic fashion.

Other principles could also be found. Both synesthetes and controls showed a tendency for letters that are the first letter of a color name to be associated with that color. Thus, Y tends to be a shade of yellow far more often than would be expected by chance; B is blue or brown, G is green, and R is red. Some letters buck the trend. Thus, O tends to be white for synesthetes but controls tend to think of orange (a verbal association between 'O' and 'orange'). However, if controls don't think of orange then white is the next most common response and they are more likely to choose white if they have to select a seen color rather than generate the name of a color. A recent study of three- to four-year-olds who have yet to learn to read and write investigated how they assigned colors to the pairs of letters O and X, and A and G. Synesthetes tend to think of O and X as white and black, whereas A and G are red and green respectively. The children were given two colored boxes (e.g. white and black), shown a letter (e.g. 'O'), and then asked to open whichever box they thought contained the same letter. For O and X, the children behaved the same as synesthetes and non-synesthetic adults by choosing white for O and black for X. This is due to the shape of the letter. If the children were shown the shape and not told the name then they chose O = white and X = black, but if they were told the name of the letter and not shown the shape they chose at random. The children also chose randomly when matching red and green to A and G, irrespective of whether they were shown the letter or told the letter name. This suggests that some synesthetic associations are based on shape (O/X) whereas others (A/G) may be based on literacy knowledge (e.g. that the word 'green' begins with G).

Finally, the Berlin and Kay order of colors that appears to be important in determining the color of alphabets may also be important for determining the color of days of the week. Some synesthetes experience colors for days and months that are not related to their spelling. For example, for some synesthetes 'Monday' and 'March' are not the color of M, despite all other words beginning with M being M-colored. This is more common for days than it is for months, presumably because the order of days is learned first. A study in Israel found that the order of the days of the week was linked to the Berlin and Kay order of colors that appear in natural languages of the world. It is to be noted that in the Hebrew calendar the last day of the week (the Sabbath) falls on a Saturday, with Sunday acting as the first day of the week.

What do we make of synesthetes who break the rules – the persons for whom A is black, O is pink, B is green, and so on? I am not sure what to make of them. Just because we can't figure out their system doesn't mean that there isn't one. There are also many variations that we just can't explain. For instance, although a high-pitched musical note will tend to trigger a lighter color it could be light pink or light yellow, and so on. The precise choice of colors appears to vary from person to person and this variability cannot necessarily be explained. But there is an internal force that is acting against total variability, i.e. the multisensory rules that dictate how our senses are linked. The rules manifest themselves in the conscious experiences of those who have synesthesia and in the unconscious biases of those who lack it.

Can synesthesia be turned off?

I recently gave an interview to a radio station in Dublin and the parting question was 'are there any drugs that people can take to make their synesthesia go away?' I had been asked the question many times before. If you have learned anything from this book then you should already be able to predict my answer: 'Synesthetes do not generally want their synesthesia taken away. What each of us perceives is the reality we know.' However, from a purely scientific point of view the question is still interesting: can synesthesia be turned off and, if so, how?

We have already encountered somebody who had their synesthesia turned off. Oliver Sacks' case, Jonathan I., lost the ability to see colors following damage to his brain sustained in a car accident. He also lost his synesthetic colors. But are there more common situations, not involving brain injury, in which synesthesia can be turned off?

In one of the first questionnaires that we distributed to a set of synesthetic volunteers, I asked people whether their synesthesia was enhanced or reduced in a variety of common situations: when stressed, sleepy, happy or depressed and after consuming alcohol or caffeine. Each of these states is known to be associated with subtly different changes in the functioning of the brain. The results were clear but not terribly exciting. The vast majority of synesthetes said that their synesthesia was unaffected by any of these situations. The few that did express a preference were evenly divided in terms of whether the effect was enhancing or reducing. The only potentially interesting trend is that more synesthetes believed that their synesthesia was enhanced when they were happy and no synesthete believed that it was reduced. This again supports the idea that synesthesia is regarded as a generally positive aspect of their persona.

Can synesthesia be turned off at will? One of the defining features of synesthesia is that it occurs automatically. That is, it *can't* be turned on or off at will. However, this is only partially true. Many synesthetes claim that they can reduce their synesthesia by ignoring it and enhance their synesthesia by attending to it. The synesthesia may always be there but often appears in the background rather than foreground of the mind. As one person puts it:

It's kind of like looking at your own nose – if you try, you can see it clearly, but you don't walk around the whole time 'seeing' your nose. But it's always there and you can see it, just that you don't unless you're attending to it.

Another analogy that I have heard is that synesthesia is like looking through a reflection in a shop window. One can see the goods behind the glass and simultaneously see the reflection of oneself on the window. Both are always present and are always seen but, at any point in time, we may be only aware of either the goods or the reflection but not both. We can switch our attention between them.

Attention is our way of filtering and selecting between the various sensory inputs that the brain receives. It is also the mechanism that determines which aspects of our senses become consciously perceived. We have all had the experience of searching for something that turned out to be right in front of us. What is going on here? Is it missed by the eyes? Is it missed by the visual parts of the brain? No, probably not. The eyes and the visual parts of the brain would almost certainly have detected it, but the information may have fallen outside of our window of attention and, hence, it would not be consciously seen. One dramatic demonstration of the way that attention limits what we perceive was conducted by Daniel Simons and Christopher Chabris. They studied a phenomenon called 'inattentional blindness'. Participants in their study were shown video clips of people playing basketball. They were required to count the number of passes between team players, which occur fairly rapidly. At the end of the test they were asked if they had noticed anything out of the ordinary. Many respondents claimed that they did not. However, during the video clip a man in a gorilla costume entered the basketball pitch, waved at the camera, and exited! The more difficult the counting task, the more attention it needs and the lower the probability that the gorilla will be detected. This occurs even though the gorilla must have been unconsciously processed. Findings such as these have important implications in everyday life. What if a pilot were to miss a flashing light that was right in front of him because he was attending to a different task?

The gold-standard test of showing that synesthesia occurs automatically is called the 'synesthetic Stroop test'. John Ridley Stroop originally devised the test, back in 1935, to show that the meaning of words is computed automatically. For instance, one cannot look at the word BLUE just as a collection of lines and curves. The word has a meaning that cannot be ignored. It has subsequently become one of the classic experiments in psychology that all students learn about. The original version of the test had nothing to do with synesthesia and works as follows. The test involves writing down a list of color names (RED, GREEN, YELLOW, etc.) but in the wrong ink color so that, for instance, RED is written in blue ink, GREEN is written in yellow ink, and YELLOW is written in red ink, and so on. The instructions are to name the color of the ink. But people are very slow to say that RED is 'blue'! Have a go. It is guaranteed to work.

Now imagine that you are a synesthete for whom A is red, B is green, C is yellow, and so on. But you are presented with A in blue ink, B in yellow ink, C in red ink, and so on. Synesthetes tend to be much slower at saying 'blue', 'yellow', and 'red' than if the letters were to be printed in the 'correct' colors for that person. This test has become one of the standard ways of testing for synesthesia. In the task, the synesthesia should be completely irrelevant. All the participant has to do is say the real color of the letter and *ignore* the synesthetic color. As such their performance should only be slowed down if the synesthesia cannot be totally ignored, and this does appear to be the case.

Seeing letters printed in the 'correct' color can often elicit feelings of rapture and amazement. Many synesthetes will never have seen text printed this way, unless they had created it themselves. But the 'wrong' colors can elicit a strong negative reaction; as one synesthete put it: 'It is wrong. It's like coming in to a room and finding all the chairs upside-down and everything out of place. I can't stand it. It is just wrong.'

If synesthesia cannot be totally ignored, can it be partly ignored? A number of studies have used variants of the Stroop task to figure out how attention affects synesthesia. Take a look at the letter in Figure 4. What do you see – Es or an F? Of course, the answer is both depending on whether your focus of attention is large (favoring F) or small (favoring Es). Now imagine that E is blue and F is green.

```
E  E  E  E  E
E
E
E  E  E  E
E
E
E
E
E
```

Figure 4 **By varying your focus of attention, this ambiguous figure can be interpreted as either Es or an F. What would a synesthete see if E were blue and F were green?**

What would such a synesthete see? Again, the answer appears to depend on their focus of attention, with color flipping between blue and green in line with their focus of attention (but they don't see a blended blue-green).

Directing attention away from letters can reduce the influence of synesthesia, similar to the phenomenon of inattentional blindness in the gorilla study. In a study by Jason Mattingley and colleagues, synesthetes were asked to find which of the diagonally opposite gaps in the diamond shown in Figure 5 is larger. In the example below, if participants are asked to consider the top-left and bottom-right diagonals then the task is quite easy (and demands little attention) but if they are asked to consider the top-right and bottom-left diagonals then the task is difficult (and demands more attention). At the same time as performing this discrimination, they also had to perform a synesthetic Stroop task. Imagine that the letter A is red for you. On some trials a 'correct' red color would appear and on other trials an 'incorrect' green color would appear. Mattingley found that there was less synesthesia (a smaller Stroop effect) when attention was diverted to the more difficult task. This occurs because there is less attention to devote to the letter when the task is more difficult. Note

Figure 5 Synesthesia for the letter A is diminished in a hard task (deciding which gap is larger: top right or bottom left) relative to an easy task (deciding which gap is larger: top left or bottom right), even though the visual stimulus presented to the eyes is the same in the two conditions. Adapted from Mattingley *et al.* (2006).

that the image presented to the eyes was physically identical in the easy and hard versions, and the A must have been either consciously or unconsciously processed.

Studies such as these demonstrate that the effects of synesthesia can be enhanced or reduced by directing attention towards or away from it (and the thing that triggers it). As such, the illusory visual experiences of synesthesia have a similar status to real visual experiences, which are also affected by attention. We may always see the tip of our nose and the reflection of ourselves in the shop window but we are not conscious of it unless we direct our attention to it. The visual parts of our brain may play an essential part in synesthetic vision as in normal vision, but whether or not we are consciously aware of the vision depends on whether we attend to it.

In this chapter, I have put various different observations together into a general model of synesthesia. At the core of the model is the notion that multisensory perception is a fundamental feature of our brains' processing of the senses. Synesthesia is not the same as regular multisensory perception (we are not all, strictly speaking, synesthetes), but it is rooted in it. For instance, there is a universal tendency to link auditory pitch and visual lightness, whether synesthetic or not. By pushing and pulling these links we may cross over into an altered sensory reality in which letters have color or music is truly psychedelic. The way in which our multisensory links are pushed and pulled depends, broadly, on whether the synesthesia is acquired or occurs naturally (with a genetic influence). However, all types of synesthesia have in common the notion that one kind of brain activity such as listening to music or counting numbers, triggers enough activity in parts of the brain that are dedicated to color, taste, etc. Like other 'real' sensory experiences, synesthesia can be enhanced or reduced by attending to it or ignoring it.

This is not yet the end of the story. Synesthesia, like other sensory experiences, exists in space. Space provides a substrate for pulling together information from the different senses. But with science, we can pull space apart in order to understand it. For example, in the next chapter I will consider the phantom limb phenomenon in which people who have amputated limbs still feel touch and pain 'out there' in the empty space that their limb used to occupy. I will also consider how space is an important property of the way that we *think* about the world. Why is December located to the right of the number 2? Why do our brains think of time and sequences in terms of space?

4

The screen in my forehead

In the first chapter, I quoted from a letter sent to me by one of our research volunteers, Debbie. She had described 40 as 'a red number with a warm feel . . . halfway up the line to 100' and her parents had looked at her as if she were an alien. Later in her letter she elaborates about how she experiences her world:

Your questionnaire made me think about it more deeply than I have done before, and I realize that I am constantly holding at least three images in my head. Firstly, what I see in front of me. Secondly, in a sort of semicircle, filling the top part of my head, but definitely inside, perhaps level with my ears, is my synesthetic image. And thirdly, anything I happen to be thinking of, such as my route home etc., which will almost be on a screen at an angle to my synesthetic screen.

For most people reading this, the descriptions are beyond comprehension. What does it mean that her synesthetic 'screen' is definitely inside 'the top part of my head'? And what does it mean to have another 'screen' that is at an angle to this? On the face of it, it seems barking mad!

But it isn't. Or, at least, I am not convinced that it is. What Debbie is describing is different spatial maps that, to her, serve different functions. In this chapter, I will argue that we all have lots of different spatial maps in our brain that serve different functions. True, they may not be the same maps that Debbie appears to be reporting and, unlike Debbie, we may not be consciously aware that different maps exist. Nevertheless, I shall argue that this is a basic design feature of our brains whether we have synesthesia or not. Synesthesia may provide a unique window into the nature of how the brain creates a sense of space.

It is virtually impossible to imagine a sensation without that sensation having a location. A touch sensation must be felt somewhere on the body, and colors don't exist free-floating. Colors are intimately bound to the surfaces of objects. We could imagine a red dot, but it would still have some extension in space. Was the dot central, to the left or right? Was it big, small, near, or far? Our perceptions of the world almost invariably have a spatial component. The same is true of synesthetic perceptions. They exist some-where, even if it can be very hard to articulate where (as with Debbie). They may be in different places for different people. Some synesthetes when they see the letter 'A' claim that there is a red color shining through the shape of the letter on the page or screen. Others may claim to see red 18 inches from their body, irrespective of how far away the letter is. Yet others claim that it is somehow in their head, literally not metaphorically, for example 'on different screens, mainly on the inside of my forehead' or 'they per-meate the center of my brain – a warm feeling about 5–8 cm square'. Some claim that they are 'just there' but are unable to take their description further.

Space is a common dimension of our different senses. Consider the end of one of your finger tips. You can see this point in space, but you can also feel it (if you wiggle the finger or touch it), and you could possibly also hear it (if you tap the table). It is for this reason that space isn't con-sidered a separate sense in its own right. It doesn't appear on the list of possible senses in Chapter 2. Space is a uni-fying feature of different sensory systems, and it provides an important substrate for linking our senses together both in synesthesia and in regular multisensory perception.

In everyday life, different maps are used to convey different information for different tasks. Most maps convey distance and directions as in a conventional A–Z street map. A third dimension can be conveyed by contours such as on an ordinance survey map, in which navigating in the third dimension is more crucial. Other maps don't convey distances, such as the famous map of the London Underground produced in 1933 by Harry Beck based on the principles of an electrical wiring diagram. Nor do all maps represent space. Historians use timelines to represent the distance, in time, between significant events. There is a map of London showing the distance in time (rather than distance in space) to walk between Underground stations, as a greener alternative to public transport. In the brain, there are different maps that serve different functions rather than just acting as passive stores of our senses. Finding our way to the local bank uses a very different map to the one that we would use for lifting a cup of tea, and this may be different still from the map we use to figure out the central letter of our first name. Similarly, our brains tend to use spatial maps to represent non-spatial concepts such as time and number in the same way as equivalent maps exist in the physical world.

The phantom touch

George Dedlow was the son of a doctor, and was training to become a doctor himself when his medical studies were cut short by the American Civil War. Even though he had not yet graduated, the army was very willing to have him as a surgeon. However, it was Dedlow himself who would ultimately fall under the surgeon's knife as, one by one, he lost every single limb. First, his right arm was hit in a rifle exchange leading to horrific pain and, ultimately, amputation. Then in 1863 in the battle of Chickamauga his legs were badly injured in shelling.

I asked the steward where I was hit, 'both thighs,' said he; 'the doctors won't do nothing.'

'No use?' said I.

'Not much,' said he.

'Not much means none at all,' I answered . . .

A moment after a steward put a towel over my mouth, and I smelled the familiar odor of chloroform, which I was glad enough to breathe . . . I awoke to consciousness in a hospital tent . . . and was suddenly aware of a sharp cramp in my left leg. I tried to get at it to rub it with my single arm, but, finding myself too weak, hailed an attendant. 'Just rub my left calf,' said I, 'if you please.'

'Calf?' said he. 'You ain't none, pardner. It's took off.'

'I know better,' said I. 'I have pain in both legs.'

'Wall, I never!' said he. 'You ain't got nary leg.'

Both legs had indeed been amputated, very high up. Dedlow was transferred to a hospital in Nashville with some 10,000 other patients. It was here that an epidemic of gangrene broke out on his ward. 'Strangely enough,' as Dedlow matter-of-factly puts it, his last remaining arm was 'seized with gangrene . . . and amputated at the shoulder joint', leaving him a 'useless torso'.

Dedlow was transferred to a number of institutions, including one with the 'not very pleasing title' of Stump Hospital. Here he observed that 'the great mass of men who had undergone amputations for many months felt the unusual consciousness that they still had the lost limb. It itched or pained, or was cramped.' This account is one of the first descriptions of a phenomenon that is now known as phantom limb. It affects almost everyone who has had an amputation at some point. The experienced sensations can differ. Some people have a sense that their arms can still move to, for example, gesticulate when talking. Others have a sense of a limb locked into position. In the First World War, many people suffered amputation when a grenade exploded prematurely in their hand. Some reported that the phantom hand was forever clasped tightly around the grenade as a painful echo of its last moments. However, all cases have one thing in common. The missing limb feels as if it still exists 'out there' in space.

Dedlow's explanation for it showed a high degree of insight. He remarked that 'the nerve is like a bell wire. You may pull it at any part of its course, and thus ring the bell as well as if you pulled it at the end of the wire.' Indeed this is so, but the phenomenon of phantom limbs almost certainly arises right at the other end of the 'wire', in the brain itself (and not the stump). Phantom limb phenomena resemble the kinds of brain restructuring that I have already noted can occur after blindness, except that the affected sense is touch (and proprioception, our sense of the position of the body in space) rather than vision. If a part of the brain fails to receive its normal inputs (e.g. due to blindness or loss of limb) it may strengthen inputs from other parts of the brain. In phantom limbs, the part of the brain that normally responds to the missing limb may respond to touch elsewhere on the body. So a touch to the face can be felt like a touch to the phantom hand as well as a touch to the face. Although phantom limb symptoms are not a true example of synesthesia, because they occur within a single sense, they illustrate a key point developed in this chapter, namely that the brain creates a feeling of our sensations existing in space even when there is nothing physically in that space to be sensed.

Intriguingly, synesthesia can play a role in modifying the phantom limb experience and may even offer a simple cure for the pain. Compared to the naturally occurring types of synesthesia, the acquired types of synesthesia have a fly-by-night quality. Recall the case of Pat Fletcher in Chapter 1, who wore a sensory substitution device that converted visual images to sounds, and her brain then converted the sounds back to synesthetic images. When the device is switched off, so is her synesthesia. An analogous situation can occur in amputees if they are presented with a visual image of their missing limb. This could be achieved by placing a plastic or prosthetic arm in the space where it feels like their phantom arm is. Or it can be achieved using a mirror such that the seen position of the reflection of their real arm coincides with the felt position of the missing arm. In these situations, it feels like their missing arm has returned. The brain is synesthetically fooled by the vision of the arm. With the phantom arm visually restored as a mirror reflection, touching the real arm can produce a duplicated touch sensation on the phantom. Movement in the real arm can also be felt in the phantom and, in some cases, is sufficient to alleviate the associated pain.

Figure 6 The participant (on the left) sees a rubber hand being stroked by the experimenter (on the right) while his/her own hidden hand is simultaneously stroked. After several minutes of stroking the participant may feel that the rubber hand is now part of their body!

This type of synesthesia-using-mirrors does not necessarily reflect a major reorganization of the senses because a similar illusion occurs in people without synesthesia and without amputated limbs. It has been termed the 'rubber hand illusion'. It works as follows, but to try it yourself you will need an accomplice (Figure 6). Place one of your own arms under a table so you can't see it. On top of the table place a fake hand, or someone else's hand. Now somebody else, your accomplice, needs to stroke both your real hidden hand and the rubber hand in synchrony with each other for a minute or two. Many people report that the rubber hand feels like it is now their hand, a kind of out-of-body experience. Like 'Thing', the disembodied hand from the Addams Family, the rubber hand feels curiously alive. Indeed, during the illusion people have difficulty in judging the true location of their hidden hand under the table, consistent with the idea that the rubber hand is effectively acting as if it was their hand. The standard explanation of this is that there are two conflicting sources of spatial information: visual information from the rubber hand and proprioceptive information from the real hand and arm. Recall from Chapter 2 that proprioception is the sense that codes the position of the joints through receptors in the muscles and ligaments. Because vision tends to be spatially more accurate, the conflict is resolved in its favor even though, in this instance, the vision is inaccurate. If one of the fingers of the rubber hand is bent back into a painful position, then people respond to the seen pain as if it is their own (they produce a sweat response).

The rubber hand illusion is not strictly a true example of synesthesia, because the illusion requires both touch and vision to be present (rather than touch triggered by vision alone), but it is almost certainly tapping the same mechanisms that give rise to the synesthesia-using-mirrors in phantom limbs. One recent variant of the experiment does, however, resemble a true instance of universal (or near-universal) synesthesia in the general population. If the rubber hand is stroked with a laser light, then two-thirds of people report thermal or tactile sensations on their hand even though the hidden hand receives no direct touch.

Different types of space

The preceding discussion has introduced the idea that there can be different spatial codes for our senses. We know the position and orientation of our limbs in space because of a proprioceptive code and this is separate from the visual spatial code derived from the pattern of light on our retina that enables us to see the location of our limbs. Other senses such as touch, pain, and hearing all have their own ways of coding space. Occasionally these different spatial codes may present conflicting information, as in the rubber hand illusion and in ventriloquism, but in general they would tend to coincide with each other and can be combined profitably.

Combining different types of spatial information, however, isn't as straightforward as it might at first seem. Imagine that you see a cup of tea on the table in front of you and you want to pick it up. A very straightforward task, it would seem. But how, exactly, do you know where it is? The pattern of light associated with the cup will stimulate one part of the retina. The retina and the earliest visual part of the brain contain a map of visual space. Objects lying on the right side of space end up on the left side of the retina and vice versa. But the crux of the problem is that you can't use just the position on the retina to figure out where in space the cup of tea lies. The eyes are constantly moving around, and the position on the retinal map would dart around too. Reaching for the cup, based on a retinal map alone, would be like catching a fly. Knowing that the cup is on the left, center or right of a retinal map is completely uninformative – unless, that is, one happens to also know the position of the eyes and head in space. If the eyes are looking twenty degrees to the left, the head is straight ahead, and the position of the cup on the retinal map is ten degrees to the right, then the direction of the cup 'out there' in external space can now be computed. You still don't have your cup of tea yet. In order to pick it up you need to know the position of your hand in space. As already discussed in the context of the rubber hand illusion, this can be determined by seeing the hand (i.e. the hand, like the cup, becomes a point on the retinal map) or using our sense of proprioception or, most likely, both.

Scientists refer to the sequence of events above in terms of coordinate transformations. As in real life, maps have different scales and origins (i.e. centers of the maps) and represent different kinds of information. To place one map on top of another would involve finding a common point of reference and adjusting the scales of the map to fit each other. The brain does the same. The origin of the retinal map is the central point of our gaze and other points are represented in terms of distance and direction from this point. However, there are also hand-centered maps in the brain in which points in space are represented in terms of distance from the hand (i.e. the position of the hand acts as the origin). In general, the coordinate transformations operate by putting the position of our eyes, head and body into a map of our current visual world. This map of the current visual world does not reside on the retina itself or even in the visual parts of the brain, but in a region of the brain that is specialized for processing space – the parietal lobes.

These coordinate transformations are an example of multisensory perception in which one type of sensory information is linked to another. For instance, it involves linking proprioceptive information about the orientation of the head (based on the stretch of muscles and ligaments in the neck) with visual information derived from the eyes. The same occurs in hearing and touch. Figuring out whether a sound is coming from the left, right or center of space not only depends on the auditory inputs to the left and right ears but also requires knowing about whether the head is oriented to the left or right. Similarly, a touch on the left hand wouldn't help you to locate the thing that is doing the touching unless you also knew where the hand was located in space. Our sense of touch just tells us which part of the body is touched. Other senses (e.g. vision, proprioception) are required to tell us where our body parts are at any given moment in time.

Synesthesia appears to be parasitic on the different maps of space that exist in the brain. I use the term 'parasitic' because the original functions of the maps are not preserved in synesthesia. In the non-synesthetic brain, different maps exist to enable us to combine the different types of spatial information required to, for instance, pick up a cup of tea that is a meter away. But we cannot pick up a synesthetic number 5 that is a meter away. The existence of different maps in synesthesia is consistent, however, with the view that I articulated earlier that synesthesia depends on altered functioning of normal processes of multisensory perception even if the original functions are not faithfully preserved.

Let's consider the common tendency of synesthetes to experience numbers, days, and months in space. Ask a synesthete where these appear in space and you could get a variety of different answers. For some synesthetes the months of the year appear like a hula-hoop around their body or a line in front of them. However, as they move their eyes or turn their head the position of the months remains fixed around their body. That is, the origin of their synesthetic map is the trunk of their body. Pat Duffy has an unusual spatial coding for her months of the year that is partly based on this principle. Her calendar is arranged around her midriff and so is positioned relative to her body. When she goes to the shops, her months go with her! However, if she rotates herself, her mental calendar does not necessarily rotate with her. It is as if the location of the form is dictated by body coordinates but the rotation of the form is partly based on external coordinates.

Other synesthetes apparently use maps with different coordinates. Francis Galton reported synesthetes who visualize the sequence of numbers arranged in space. He called these 'number forms'. For one of these people, the origin of the map was the position of the head rather than the trunk of the body.

The diagram of the numerals has roughly the shape of a horseshoe, lying on a slightly inclined plane with the open end towards me; zero is in front of my left eye. When I move my eyes without moving my head, the diagram remains fixed in space and does not follow the movement of my eye. When I move the head, the diagram unconsciously follows the movement.

Yet other synesthetes experience numbers or the calendar in their 'mind's eye', which is typically described as like an inner screen but is defined in coordinates that are independent of body parts.

For synesthetes who experience colors when they see letters or numbers on a page or on a computer screen, there are different types of spatial experience corresponding to different maps in the brain. Mike Dixon and colleagues in Canada have referred to them as 'projectors' and 'associators'. For projectors, looking at a letter on a computer screen such as 'A' may trigger a sensation of color, such as red, that is located 'out there' as if it is literally superimposed on or shining through the screen. The synesthetes still claim to be able to see the true color of the letter (i.e.

black) but it coexists with the synesthetic color. It is very hard to imagine what this feels like, but perhaps it is comparable to the example of the big F made up of little Es in Chapter 3 (Figure 4). They coexist but you can, to some extent, choose which one to attend to. Zanna, a projector synesthete, describes it as follows:

For me it's as though the text is literally printed in my colors. Regardless of the actual color of the text, the letters quite happily 'appear' as both the real and synesthetic colors at the same time – though even I can see how ridiculous that sounds! Things like the Roman numeral 'IV' can even appear as a whole host of colors simultaneously: the real color of the text, a green four, and a black I with a brown V.

Associators, on the other hand, report seeing their colors internally in their mind's eye. The most common way of describing it is that when they look at 'A' on the computer screen they see it as black on white but they see another copy of the letter in a different spatial location (their mind's eye) that is colored, say, red.

The validity of these subtypes is demonstrated in a number of experiments. When presented with colored letters, associators are faster at saying the real color of the letter (i.e. the color it is really printed in) than at saying their synesthetic color. For projector synesthetes, the reverse is true. They can be faster at saying that a green-colored A is red (their synesthetic color) than saying that it is green (the real color). It is as if the synesthetic color partially obscures or is more vivid than the real color. However, in associator synesthetes their synesthetic color is in a different spatial location to the real color. Saying their synesthetic color would presumably involve attending to the letter 'out there' and then switching their attention to the color 'in here' (for projector synesthetes both the color and the letter are 'out there'). A briefly flashed letter on the edge of their vision is more likely to be described as colored by a projector than an associator, although they don't necessarily see the correct color unless the letter itself is also consciously seen.

The problem with the projector–associator distinction is that it doesn't go far enough. The typical projector sees their synesthetic color on the page, on the computer screen or wherever the letter is (and irrespective of whether they look straight at it or over their shoulder at it). That is, the origin of their synesthetic map is centered on the words themselves. However, some synesthetes see colors in external space but not bound to the letters. For example, one of the synesthetes that I have worked with, Michelle, experiences colors on a 'screen' that is about 18 inches in front of her body. When she reads or hears someone speaking the words are spelled out in glorious Technicolor on her screen, like the news headlines in Time Square. Another person, Elizabeth, has something similar except that her screen is above her right shoulder! Both Michelle and Elizabeth have the origin of their synesthetic map defined relative to their bodies. Thus the claim that projector synesthetes see their synesthetic colors 'out there' in external space fails to recognize that there are different maps of external space: including maps with their origin centered on the body, and maps that are centered on the location of seen objects such as letters. The two types of projector behave differently on the experiments described above. It is the precise nature of the spatial map that is important rather than the distinction between externalized colors versus an internal 'mind's eye'.

There are other types of map that fall between the cracks of the projector–associator distinction. As already noted, some synesthetes literally claim that colors lie inside their body. An 1893 review in the medical journal *The Lancet* considered some four types of location for synesthetic experiences, including 'somewhere behind the eyes or within the skull'. There is a case of colored taste in which the experienced colors were located inside the mouth. Given that synesthesia does not depend on the eyes, there is no logical reason why synesthetic colors couldn't be found in locations in the mouth or behind the eyes. But most of us cannot begin to comprehend what that must be like.

Although most of the evidence comes from colored letters or from experiences of time or number in space, there is much anecdotal evidence that these different spatial maps exist in other types of synesthesia. When one is hearing music or speech, the color of the sounds often lies on screens defined relative to the head or body, or on some inner screen, but it can also come from the location of the sound source itself in some people. Thus, a sudden ring of the phone to the left and behind them may trigger a color that originates in the direction of the sound (i.e. the location of this synesthetic map has an origin based on the location of the sound). For one remarkable person that I have met, Suzanne, when she sees someone talking, written words appear to literally fall out of their mouths! The words trail away moving right and downwards, like the speech of comic books. Something akin to the projector–associator distinction can be found for other types of synesthesia such as colored taste and colored smell. For some synesthetes, colored smells may appear externally like a psychedelic mist ('like the bits in *Lord of the Rings* where Frodo puts the ring on'), but many people with colored smell see them internally in the mind's eye.

One unusual type of projected color experience is where colors are seen as emanating from someone's head, or body, like an aura. Many of the cases that I have heard about have been in younger people, suggesting that it may be more common in children. One ten-year-old girl, Matilda, commented that 'I see the colors of people and animals as if the color is there around their heads, *not* in my mind. I see a spiky circle of colored light about half a centimeter deep around their head. The color varies with my feelings about them. Strangers are gray.' Matilda also has more 'normal' types of synesthesia including colored music, letters and numbers. Interestingly, her colored auras have faded since she initially contacted me, although her other types of synesthesia remain strong. Another feature of this type of synesthesia is that the color appears to depend on the personality of the person they are looking at, and how familiar they are with that person. I have suggested that this may relate to the way that the perceiver reacts, emotionally, to the people around them. Another seven-year-old synesthete remarked that strangers were 'bright orange with a black outline . . . As I know them better they get mild blue or pinkish orchid . . . When I know people well they stop changing colors; they are the color.' When he was taken to watch *Oliver Twist* at the cinema, Fagin and the Artful Dodger were black, Oliver was light blue, Nancy was red or green, and so on. One month later, when asked to categorize colored yarns according to pleasantness, his groupings were appropriate to the previous characterizations.

These descriptions of auras 'out there' around the face and body bear obvious resemblance to those described in books on the occult or mysticism. These are normally 'explained' in terms of hidden energies that everyone emits but only a few people perceive. I argue that nobody emits hidden energies but a few people are able to synesthetically convert their own emotional response to another person into color experiences. The emotional response depends on the perceived personality, such as whether they are calm or pleasant. The colors themselves seem to emanate externally in space but that itself is no mystery, it just depends on the map that is being used. An explanation in terms of synesthesia is the first scientifically credible account of this phenomenon. There are also books out there that claim to train people who lack synesthesia to 'tune in' to the hidden energies and see the aura of other people. I am dubious of these claims. I don't believe that synesthesia can be learned like this and I don't believe that there is a hidden energy that can be tuned into. However, I am willing to stick my neck out and claim that some cases in which those perceiving the auras have no obvious training could be genuine cases of synesthesia.

Acquired types of synesthesia may also utilize some of these different maps although they have not been extensively documented. Some cases of synesthesia have been observed in partial blindness. For example, partial damage to the optic nerve, which carries information from the eyes to the brain, can result in localized blind spots. Some synesthetes experience synesthetic vision, from sound, that is limited to this blind spot so that when they move their eyes the location of the synesthesia moves with it – a map based on retinal positions. The missing regions of the visual map of the retina in the brain get filled-in by inputs from hearing. One case of synesthesia following blindness experienced vision from touch. The location of the synesthesia depended on the location of the body part (i.e. it must have used proprioceptive information), so, for example, taps to the left hand would trigger jumping lights in the location of the hand irrespective of whether the left hand was on the left or the right side of space. However, if the hand was held behind the head then greater pressure was needed to produce the visual experiences. Thus, synesthetic vision was harder to trigger behind the head than in front of it, even though the person was blind. Information from one sense (proprioception) was modulating another sense (synesthetic vision).

A space to think

I suggested above that the different spatial maps found in synesthesia do not preserve the original functions of these maps. However, this does not mean that they don't have any function at all. The ability to represent concepts spatially, such as time and number, could itself have certain benefits. Remembering things spatially also has known benefits on memory and this could be a fortuitous consequence of this aspect of synesthesia.

The extent to which people think visually and spatially varies considerably within the general population. I tend not to think this way at all and, for me, reading a book is just like a narrative and does not resemble an inner movie or picture. Many people, whether synesthetic or not, would disagree vehemently with this. If a friend or a situation is described, then they would easily visualize that friend and that situation. The location of the images can also differ. Up to a quarter of children before the age of seven years project visual images into the space in front of them, whereas the vast majority of other people would describe it more like an inner screen within their mind's eye. People with synesthesia subjectively report more vivid visual imagery than the rest of the population when asked to rate how clear and vivid a mental image of, say, a shopfront is. However, I don't think that synesthetic experiences are identical to normal vivid imagery. Normal imagery is flexible and can be controlled at will: one can imagine a friend's face in profile or face-on, or wearing a hat or fake moustache, or we can normally make the face go away completely. Synesthetic experiences are certain: for example, an A is always red and an O is always white. Nevertheless both synesthesia and normal vivid imagery do have something in common: both represent instances in which our inner thoughts manifest themselves in sensory and spatial codes.

All of us are capable of thinking spatially even if we are not consciously aware of doing so. Even concepts that are not inherently spatial may be imbued with spatial codes. The question of how the brain is able to comprehend abstract concepts such as number and time has always been a puzzle. One solution is to make them more concrete by giving them properties of sensed objects. A number such as 'three' is abstract insofar as it can refer to any collection of three: three elephants, three sounds, three ideas, and so on. Stanislas Dehaene, of the University of Paris, has argued that everybody possesses a 'mental number line' that enables us to understand numbers. He argues that the way that the brain understands numbers is equivalent to the way that it understands physical dimensions such as length. If two lines are shown and we are asked to decide which is longer, the brain finds it easier if the difference between them is greater (e.g. lines of 3 cm v. 7 cm are easier to discriminate than 3 cm v. 5 cm) or they are shorter (e.g. lines of 3 cm v. 5 cm are easier to discriminate than 5 cm v. 7 cm). Interestingly, the same occurs if pairs of digits are presented instead of physical lines. Moreover, he argues that the mental number line has a spatial dimension to it such that, at least in Western cultures, the line is oriented from left to right. Smaller numbers appear on the left and larger numbers on the right.

There is good evidence that numbers possess a spatial code. Imagine an experiment in which a digit appears on the center of the computer screen and we have to decide whether it is odd or even by pressing a button on the left or right (some people are instructed to press left for odd and right for even, and others are told the reverse). In this task, we are faster at responding to smaller numbers (e.g. 1 and 2) with our left hand and faster at responding to larger numbers (e.g. 8 and 9) with our right hand. Intermediate numbers fall between. It is as if there is a spatially oriented number line outside of our body that unconsciously biases our speed of responding to numbers. It is not to do with handedness: left- and right-handed people behave similarly on the task. Nor is it to do with the position of the hands: if the hands are crossed such that the left hand is on the right and the right hand is on the left, the number line does not reverse in direction. In the jargon used above, our map of numbers has its reference point (i.e. the origin) in the body rather than the hands. The direction may, however, be biased by reading direction. Persian immigrants to Paris showed a reduced effect depending on the length of time they have lived in the west.

Synesthetes often consciously experience numbers that are organized spatially. As many as 12 percent of the population have this type of synesthesia. Perhaps these number sequences are the consciously seen versions of the mental number line that we all seem to have unconsciously. Most of these number sequences tend to be arranged roughly in a left to right orientation, although even in Western cultures some people have it going right to left, or vertically, or even in spirals. For some synesthetes, the numbers can be scrolled through space. So to 'get' a large number they would scroll along the line in front of them until it appeared near by. Other synesthetes report fixed viewpoints from which they view the numbers and can hop from viewpoint to viewpoint depending on the number they are searching for.

Are spatial number forms a benefit or a hindrance to calculation? Most people who have a number form claim to use it in some types of calculation. However, there is little evidence that it conveys either a benefit or a problem. It may just be an alternative way of getting an answer. We recently gave a large group of synesthetes easy arithmetic problems of addition, subtraction, and multiplication and they had to give the answer as quickly as possible. There were no differences on addition and subtraction. Those synesthetes with number forms were actually slower (but just as accurate) on multiplication than synesthetes without a number form, perhaps because they had 'further to go' on their number form to retrieve the answer, whereas for other people the answer was perhaps retrieved as a nonspatial verbal fact. Synesthesia could also be an important aid for memorizing numbers (e.g. a phone number or the decimal places of pi, 3.142 . . .); I'll come back to this point later in the chapter.

If numbers trigger colors then the color may become part of the meaning of that number. Mike Dixon and colleagues conducted a study entitled 'Five plus two equals yellow'. Their synesthete was shown arithmetical sums (e.g. $5 + 2$) followed by a color that she had to say. The synesthete experiences the number 7 as yellow, but the number 7 was not physically presented to her, it was only ever implied. However, she was faster at saying the color yellow than other colors. This suggests that the *thought* of the number seven is sufficient to trigger the color yellow. Another study on a different synesthete presented colored lines, with the colors coincidentally corresponding to the colors of digits. The synesthete was faster at spotting the longer line if the colors implied a large difference (e.g. a line in the color of 2 v. a line in the color of 9) relative to a small difference (e.g. a line in the color of 2 v. a line in the color of 3). This again suggests that a color can imply a number, as well as vice versa.

Aside from numbers, the most commonly reported spatial synesthesia involves time. This normally involves the days of the week and months of the year. A new week is often added to the old week, creating an infinitely repeating series of seven blocks. Sometimes the days of the week or months of the year link together in a circle, like a snake eating its tail. Saturdays and Sundays and special months of the year often occupy a greater portion of space as if to enable its user to fit more activities into them (see Figure 7).

The synesthesia can also involve times of day and even epochs of history. Rachel, one of the synesthetes I'll consider in more detail below, reports the following:

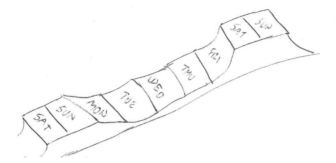

Figure 7 **Claire experiences her days of the week as a continuous spatial landscape in front of her.**

The standard timeline of my life, and past history relating to dates and periods, is on the right stretching down about a foot from my body; the dark ages are about thigh/knee level. History curves round onto an infinite dark plane around the start of AD. BC definitely goes left and becomes totally horizontal space around my shins but with the dimensions of a vast plane and not near my body.

As with numbers, there is some evidence that we all code time spatially. Spatial metaphors of time are commonplace: the future lies ahead of us; the past is behind us. As with numbers, people are faster at making judgments about early months (January, February, etc.) with their left hand and faster at making judgments about later months (e.g. November, December) with their right hands, as if they possess a mental calendar laid out from left to right in front of them.

Almost all synesthetes claim that this comes in very useful for remembering dates and appointments. One of the most extraordinary synesthetes that I have worked with, Andrew, has an amazing memory and is particularly good with dates. He often surprises casual acquaintances by saying 'Happy Birthday' on the correct date, or by figuring out that they are lying about their age if they say they were born on a Tuesday (and he knows that day to be Wednesday). He is able to 'calendar count', which refers to the ability to translate a given date (e.g. February 2 1972) into a day of the week (a Wednesday). He does this synesthetic-ally using the following method. He has memorized the days of certain points in time, such as his birth date and that of other family members, and these serve as anchor points. To figure out the day of the week for a date that he hasn't memorized he would choose a nearby anchor point and then spatially scroll along his timeline, week by week, until the correct date is found at which point he can read off the answer as a 'Saturday' or whatever it turns out to be.

The tendency to think spatially is by no means limited to numbers and time. Rachel, who described her historical timeline above, is a mapmaker extraordinaire. After filling in our questionnaire, which asked only about numbers, letters and time, she noted many other things that were organized spatially. These included numbers, letters of the alphabet, time (separate forms for days of the week, months of the year, time within the day, years and historical periods), percentages, human height, shoe sizes, distances, weight (kilos, stones, ounces and pounds all being separate in space), temperature (Celcius and Fahrenheit), and cur-rency (decimal versus pre-decimal)! Over a Christmas break she took the trouble of sketching them all down on the back of a four or five meter roll of paper that I still have in my office.

There are various planes: horizontal, vertical, starting on the left, starting on the right, above waist level, below waist level, and stretching out in front of me. The alphabet is pretty much upright but [the letters are] variable sizes and veers off a bit upwards right, and away from me after QRST . . . Months of the year twist a bit and move depending on the starting month I am thinking about . . . Weeks have several forms starting on a basic Sun–Mon in front of me left to right . . . All these subjects are in completely separate planes. Nothing shares the same space . . . I suddenly realize how fixed and definite it all is and am surprised that you don't know where these things are.

The space around her body is cluttered with synesthetic sequences and maps. One would imagine that seeing past all these things would make her vision difficult. But, as with other types of synesthesia, her spatial forms only enter her awareness when she thinks about time, numbers, or whatever, at which point each magically reappears in its own unique position (in the same way as we don't see the end of our nose unless we look for it). She is adamant that she does not deliberately invent them. Rather, her brain constructs them whenever she deals with new sequences. Her parietal lobes must have been working overtime. The spatial forms are capable of being modified under some circumstances, as she notes for her spatial representation of temperature.

About 20 years ago I moved to Japan. Until then I had always understood temperature in Fahrenheit, but had to adapt to a new hotter climate and using centigrade. I realize now that these two systems have two different planes and the Fahrenheit one that I no longer use has dimmed, it has become very low down as an image and in the distance; only 32 [freezing point] has a really strong position. The focal point of the centigrade system is around 30 degrees as we moved in early summer and had to get to grips with higher temperatures.

Procedures as well as sequences become visualized spatially. She describes using a Macintosh computer as like navigating in an open-plan office, but a PC has lots of wall-like barriers in the landscape. For baking a cake, each step in the process has a three-dimensional spatial element to it. She has a sensation of journeying over a landscape as she bakes, and the difficult bits are represented as vertical barriers that she feels that she has to travel up and over. She insists: 'This is not a metaphor but a physical landscape.' Other concepts that are neither sequential nor inherently spatial are represented spatially by her brain. She describes how authors, artists and composers are arranged geographically in a warped map of the world that she has the sensation of looking down upon.

Authors, composers and artists hover over Europe (not together, a different empty map for each group), which is a massive expanse on a horizontal plane on the right, but I am above it a bit to the left of Brittany looking down at a 45 degree angle. It all becomes vertical and more to the left below Israel. Africa is on a completely vertical plane.

The brain has an extraordinary ability to construct organized systems and structures out of the information it is given. Synesthesia gives people a rich source of extra information and this becomes assimilated into their thought processes. In Rachel's case, her brain has an extraordinary ability to construct spatial maps that guide her thoughts about the world. One of the remaining themes that I want to develop in this book is how synesthesia is more than just an altered way of perceiving the world – it is an altered way of thinking about and interacting with the world. I will start to develop this theme in the section below and will return to it in detail in the final chapter.

The pi man

On March 14 2004, Daniel Tammet broke the European record for reciting 22,514 digits of pi without error in the time of 5 hours and 9 minutes. Pi is the Greek letter that denotes the ratio of a circle's circumference to its diameter. March 14 is, apparently, International Pi Day because the date in US notation is 3/14, corresponding to the first two decimal places of this celebrated number (3.1416 . . .). Pi is an infinite number and an irregular number. It cannot be expressed as a simple fraction of two whole numbers and the next number in the sequence of decimal places is entirely unpredictable. How did Daniel remember the sequence? This is how he describes it:

When I look at a sequence of numbers, my head begins to fill with colors, shapes and textures that knit together spontaneously to form a visual landscape . . . To recall each digit, I simply retrace the different shapes and textures in my head and read the numbers out of them. For very long numbers, such as pi, I break the digits down into smaller segments. The size of each segment varies, depending on what the digits are. For example, if a number is very bright in my head and the next one is very dark, I would visualize them separately, whereas a smooth number followed by another smooth number would be remembered together . . . The most famous sequence of numbers in pi is the 'Feynman point' which comprises the 762nd through 767th decimal places of pi: '. . . 999999 . . .'. It is named after the physicist Richard Feynman for his remark that he would like to memorize the digits of pi as far as that point; when reciting them, he would be able to finish with: '. . . nine, nine, nine, nine, nine, nine, and so on'. The Feynman point is visually very beautiful to me; I see it as a deep, thick rim of dark blue light.

Daniel Tammet, like Richard Feynman, has synesthesia. He is able to use this to knit together different synesthetic experiences of digits into a spatial landscape. The flow of the landscape gives clues to the underlying digits. He had spent three months learning different sections of the sequence although he had never before attempted to recall it all in one go. The first 100 digits of pi are visualized as shown in Figure 8.

Daniel is capable of other remarkable feats. As part of the making of a documentary aired on British and American TV called *Brainman*, he learned to speak Icelandic in only one week. At the end of his training, his test was to take part in a live television interview – in Icelandic. He had previously taught himself Lithuanian on a teaching placement in a school there, and he now speaks ten languages. Daniel explained to me that the brain loves patterns and getting inside a language is like grasping these patterns. Synesthesia provides one easy way of tuning in to the patterns of sounds and letters that exist within a word and between words. Indeed, many synesthetes report that learning languages is one of their strengths. Daniel has subsequently set up a company that helps people to learn languages more intuitively.

Daniel not only has synesthesia, he is also autistic. Autism is a biological difficulty in socialization such that the feelings, thoughts and actions of other people are hard to interpret and predict. People with autism like routines and they like order. Daniel eats 45 grams of porridge in the

Figure 8 Daniel Tammet visualizes the first 100 digits of pi as an undulating colored spatial landscape. He can use the landscape to remember the associated digits. Reprinted with permission from Tammet (2006).

morning, and he weighs it with an electronic scale to be certain. Many autistic people are drawn to the patterns and orderliness of numbers and around 10 percent of autistic people have exceptional abilities in domains such as memory, calculation, or drawing. Daniel is also capable of performing remarkable calculations such as dividing two numbers to almost 100 decimal places. His autism probably triggers his love and zeal for numbers, but his synesthesia is also tightly bound up with his experiences when calculating:

I see thirty-seven's fifth power – $37 \times 37 \times 37 \times 37 \times 37 = 69,343,957$ – as a large circle composed of smaller circles running clockwise from the top round . . . I never write anything down when I'm calculating, because I've always been able to do the sums in my head and it's much easier for me to visualize the answer using my synesthetic shapes than to try to follow the 'carry the one' technique.

I am often asked whether I think that there is a link between synesthesia and autism, and my usual answer is 'no' (although in reality there is no research yet conducted that speaks to the question). A rare trait such as synesthesia always attracts the possible association of other rare traits, starting with albinism in 1812 and including such things as left-handedness (another myth) along the way. However, there will always be a few rare individuals who coincidentally have both synesthesia and autism and when they do, such as in Daniel's case, there could be a synergy between them. Daniel's synesthesia gives him a rich visuospatial memory and his autism gives him an unusual zeal for numbers and patterns. The two are combined with startling consequences.

Daniel is an exceptional individual. However, the use of spatial imagery as a technique to improve memory is more commonplace. It was noted by Aristotle in classical times and is known as the 'method of loci' (pronounced 'low-sigh'). The method works as follows. Imagine that you have to remember the order of a pack of cards – a favorite game of memory showmen. First of all, you need to imagine a well-known route such as my old walk from Kings Cross Thameslink station to my office in London. From the station, I walk past the ATMs, the newspaper shop, the café, the nightclub, the crossing at the traffic lights and so on. In each of these locations, I deposit a card – the five of hearts, the queen of clubs and so on. To recall the sequence you mentally walk along the familiar route and retrieve the cards. It would even be possible to recall the sequence backwards by reversing the route. Memory experts who rely on this well-established method can perform amazing feats, but they don't necessarily perform well on laboratory tests of memory that the method can't be used for. For instance, they perform no better on memorizing patterns of snowflakes that are very hard to verbalize.

Many people with synesthesia do not need to use a familiar route, as in the method of loci, because their brain is naturally adept at creating spatial landscapes and colored patterns. Synesthetes that I have spoken to tend to remember telephone numbers by visualizing the sequence of colored digits which are arranged left-to-right in stripes of color. Very few people without synesthesia claim to remember a phone number by 'seeing' a mental image of it. As with many trained memory experts, the memory of synesthetes is not necessarily globally superior. Daniel Tammet does not believe that his memory is superior in all respects, nor does he believe that it is 'photographic'. He described it to me as 'islands of ability' that center primarily on his love of numbers. As with other people with autism, he is little interested in faces and he believes that his memory for faces is poor. He often equates people with numbers so, for example, a tall person may remind him of the number 9 (this number being synesthetically tall). Although he is able to vividly remember the landscape of pi, he reports difficulties in remembering routes around the real world.

Perhaps the most well-known case of exceptional memory in a synesthete is that of Solomon Shereshevskii, who was studied by Aleksander Luria for several decades beginning in the 1920s. Shereshevskii was working for a Moscow newspaper when he came to the attention of his editor because he never took written notes of addresses, quotes or stories. He ultimately became a professional memory expert, a mnemonist, giving stage performances. In a typical experiment, he was presented with random grids of numbers as below.

6	6	8	0
5	4	3	2
1	6	8	4
7	9	3	5
4	2	3	7
3	8	9	1
1	0	0	2
3	4	5	1
2	7	6	8
1	9	2	6
2	9	6	7
5	5	2	0
x	0	1	x

He spent three minutes examining the table, and it took him 40 seconds to reproduce it. He could quite easily 'read off' the numbers in the diagonals (the groups of 4 numbers) or the vertical columns. He could still recall the grid after several months.

Shereshevskii has a more diverse range of types of synesthesia than Daniel Tammet and this is likely to have provided an extra boost to his multisensory memories. For him, sounds elicit sensations in at least three other senses: touch, taste and vision. A 2000 hertz tone at 113 decibels looked something like fireworks tinged with a pink-red hue, felt rough and unpleasant, and had the taste of a briny pickle.

Shereshevskii's skill was almost certainly attributable to two influences. Firstly, there was the influence of his synesthesia, which could be construed as a natural 'gift' to remember things in a multisensory code. Secondly, he had engaged in extensive training of his memory and he had developed sophisticated mnemonic techniques to help him. This included the well-known method of loci and also a strategy of remembering meaningless material by making it meaningful. In June 1936 he was presented with the most difficult material that he had ever been asked to memorize during a performance. It consisted of a long list of meaningless repeating syllables that were read aloud to him – 'ma, va, na, sa, na, va, na, sa, na, ma, va, sa, na, ma, va, na . . .' and so on. Most people find it extremely difficult to remember words if they sound similar, even if the words have meaning and the list is short (e.g. try these five words: 'pat, mat, cap, cat, map'). At the start of his attempt to learn the list, Shereshevskii spontaneously relied on his synesthesia. He saw an extremely thin greyish-yellow line that was related to the fact that all the vowels were A. He then saw 'lumps, splashes, blurs, bunches, all of different colors, weights and thicknesses' appear on the line that corresponded to the different consonants. The colored line would switch direction as the reader paused to begin another section of the list. This spontaneous use of a spatial map to represent a sequence is highly characteristic of synesthesia, as already noted. However, as soon as he realized that the list would continue like this he felt a sinking feeling that it would take him too long to recall it if he had to decode each synesthetic splash and lump. As such, he switched to a mnemonic technique. He grouped the meaningless syllables into the closest meaningful words that he could think of, relying on his knowledge of Russian, Yiddish, Polish, and Latvian (e.g. 'nava' is a Yiddish expression). Shereshevskii reproduced the list flawlessly. He did so again, without prior warning, some four and eight years later.

This chapter has weaved a path from perception through imagery to memory – with space acting as the common underlying thread. Space is a vital aspect of the way that we link our senses together, and is essential for linking our perceptions of the world with our actions upon it. Space exists in multiple maps in the brain that are recruited to serve different functions. Synesthesia, like other sensory experiences, has a spatial dimension and synesthesia resides in the various different maps of the brain. Space is a convenient medium not only for representing physical distances in the sensory world but also for representing distances in time and for representing arbitrary sequences such as those learned in memory experiments and those that guide day-to-day behavior such as baking a cake. People with synesthesia are often consciously aware of such spatial relationships, but they are also present, to some degree, in everyone.

The discussion has taken me away from considering synesthesia as a purely sensory experience to being tied in with the way that we think about the world – our understanding of numbers and time, our use of language (e.g. why 'high pitch' is high), and our ability to remember. The final chapter will consider in more detail synesthesia's role beyond the senses.

5

Beyond the senses

This chapter asks some big questions. Why does synesthesia exist? Does it have any advantages? Did it evolve for a particular reason? As such, the discussion will focus on the developmental variety of synesthesia that is known to have a genetic component. Synesthesia is defined in terms of unusual sensory experiences, and I have argued that this has its roots in the kind of multisensory perception that we all continually engage in. Although this is fascinating in its own right, perhaps it is a red herring in terms of the bigger picture. For instance, one widely publicized claim is that synesthesia could exist to permit human creativity. Under this account, the actual sensory experiences are a by-product – a colorful sideshow – of synesthesia's real purpose in life. I will cast a critical eye over this and other claims.

A survey of 192 synesthetes recently conducted in Australia asked them to specify their strengths and weaknesses. The question was open-ended so that they weren't prompted to think of particular answers. The question was also put to a control group of people of similar age as a comparison. The following list gives a summary of items that were noted as strengths or weaknesses significantly more often by the synesthetes than the control group.

Surveys such as this provide important clues about where to start looking, although the final answer may well turn out to be quite different. In the previous chapter, I considered how synesthesia could benefit memory. I will pick up this theme in the present chapter because I regard

Strengths	Weaknesses
Memory	Sense of direction
Languages	Coordination/balance
Writing and verbal communication	Maths
Art	
Maths	

memory as being a strong candidate for explaining why synesthesia exists in evolutionary terms. In my opinion, any advantage that synesthetes have in learning languages is also probably attributable to the benefits of synesthesia on memory. I am not aware of research on communication (written and verbal), although I will examine claims about language evolution below. Ditto for art. Maths is curious because some synesthetes claim that it is a strength but far more claim it to be a weakness. Maths has several different elements that could contribute to this confusion. Are the problems due to learning number facts (e.g. $7 \times 7 = 49$), due to a core problem with numbers themselves, or due to problems with more abstract mathematical concepts (e.g. algebra)? For instance, the synesthete Daniel Tammet, who is a prodigious human calculator, does not excel at algebra and so he opted not to study maths beyond age 16.

We recently assessed the arithmetical abilities of a large group of synesthetes, looking at single digit addition, subtraction, and multiplication. Synesthetes were two to three times as likely to demonstrate problems on these very basic tasks as a control group, although the majority of synesthetes did not have any problems in this area. The other weaknesses that synesthetes report (sense of direction and coordination/balance) have not been studied in detail. Together with problems in calculation, these have been linked to functioning of a particular region of the brain called the parietal lobes, and maybe this region does not mature normally in some synesthetes. However, any weaknesses may be offset by their potential strengths.

As a scientist, I am interested in mechanisms (e.g. why might synesthesia be related to art?) rather than the headlines that might interest a journalist (e.g. 'synesthesia is related to art'). In Chapter 3 I outlined the problem of linking synesthesia to non-sensory consequences. The problem is that there are two ways in which they could be linked and these haven't always been untangled. Are the consequences of having synesthesia related to the fact that the brains of people with synesthesia are different (and the sensory experiences are something of a sideshow) or are the consequences of having synesthesia directly related to the unusual sensory experiences themselves? Consider art. Is art a strength for synesthetes because of their beautiful sensory experiences, or because synesthetic brains are wired in a particular way irrespective of the nature of their synesthesia? I suggest that one way of disentangling this is to compare different types of synesthesia. Does an artistic inclination depend on the particular type of experience (e.g. visualized music versus tasting words) or just on being a synesthete?

I shall begin by considering our sense of touch. Touch is useful beyond its purely sensory role. It may enable us to empathize and connect with other people in social settings. Some recent clues about this have come from a newly discovered type of synesthesia. A couple of years ago, I sent an email to our new intake of undergraduate students asking if anyone had synesthesia. This was the first reply that I got from this batch of students: 'I think I might have synesthesia. I can feel touch just by looking at someone being touched.'

A touching sight

If you see someone being slapped do you literally experience a tactile sensation on your own face? For the majority of people the answer is a clear 'no'. Perhaps there was some hesitation in giving the answer as we can all imagine what this would feel like, even if we don't literally feel anything. We all have a tendency to wince and flinch when watching someone being kicked or hurt. However, people with 'mirror-touch' synesthesia literally report localized touch sensations on their own body when watching someone else being touched. This fascinating type of synesthesia is providing important clues about the wider role of touch, beyond its sensory function.

Look up the definition of touch in a dictionary or on the web and you will find more than one meaning. There is a physical, sensory meaning such as 'To cause or permit a part of the body, especially the hand or fingers, to come in contact with so as to feel'. However, there is also an affective, emotional sense in which the word is used: 'To affect the emotions of; move to tender response: "an appeal that touched us deeply".' This is probably not a coincidence. Touch is the most social and emotional sense that we have. Every culture establishes rules that govern when touch is and isn't permissible, and societies dictate the type of touch that is appropriate in a particular situation. Do we kiss, shake hands, hug or rub noses? There was outrage in the British press when the Australian Prime Minister, Paul Keating, touched the Queen on her lower back. He was dubbed the 'Lizard of Oz' for his transgression. Bill Clinton in his autobiography described the negotiations between Yasser Arafat and Yitzhak Rabin as to how they would touch each other to cement their Middle East peace agreement:

Then there was the question of whether Rabin and Arafat would shake hands. I knew Arafat wanted to do it . . . I told Yitzhak that if he was really committed to peace, he'd have to shake Arafat's hand to prove it, 'The whole world will be watching, and the handshake is what they will be looking for.' Rabin sighed, and in his deep, world-weary voice, said, 'I suppose one does not make peace with one's friends.' 'Then you'll do it?' I asked. He almost snapped at me, 'All right. All right. But no kissing.' The traditional Arab greeting was a kiss on the cheek, and he wanted no part of that.

What evidence is there that our sense of touch has an emotional role, particularly in social contexts? Apes and monkeys spend a huge amount of time grooming each other. However, it is no longer believed that they do this for the benefit of hygiene. If it was for hygiene they could groom themselves like cats. As one headline explained –

'Junkie monkeys get a quick fix from grooming'. A study by Barry Keverne in Cambridge has measured the levels of endorphins in the cerebrospinal fluid (the liquid that surrounds the brain) after grooming. Endorphins are the brain's naturally occurring opiates and they have a similar chemical structure to heroin and morphine. Social interaction, via grooming, increases the endorphin levels. The monkeys get blissed-out and group attachments and allegiances become established.

Another property of our sense of touch that may promote the social dimension is the fact that being touched by someone else elicits a greater brain response than if you touch yourself, even when all things are equal (e.g. the amount of pressure exerted). The explanation of this interesting finding is that our brains can predict what the touch will feel like when we touch ourselves, and we compensate accordingly by reducing the intensity of the sensation. But we can't do so when we are touched by someone else because we can't predict how much pressure will be applied, how long for, and whether it will be a stroke or scratch. This brain mechanism probably didn't arise for social reasons (it may enable us to give more attention to externally derived touch by making it more sensitive), but it does have potential social consequences.

What does mirror-touch synesthesia contribute to this debate? It is one of the best examples of a type of synesthesia that is an over-active version of normal multisensory perception. As such we can use it as a tool to investigate how natural variations in a 'mirror-touch' system contribute to social behavior. Our first investigation of this type of synesthesia involved brain imaging. We showed movie clips of people being touched on their faces and necks while observing which parts of the brain were most active. We compared 12 control participants, who lacked mirror-touch synesthesia, with one of our synesthetes, Christine. The results from the control participants were fascinating in their own right. The part of the brain that normally responds to actual touch was activated when the controls watched other people being touched. In other words, a purely visual stimulus activated parts of the brain specialized for touch.

The same result was found in the mirror-touch synesthete, but this brain region was far more active for Christine than for any of our controls. It was as if her brain had been over-activated to produce a conscious (i.e. synesthetic) experience of touch but it was still using the same circuitry that works unconsciously when others see touch. The result was specific to humans being touched, as her brain's response was comparable to the control group when objects (e.g. a vase) were touched. Christine does not feel touch when she sees objects being touched.

In effect, synesthetes such as Christine are literally sharing other people's sensations, and we wondered what consequences this might have in their everyday life. It could easily make them more squeamish. As one of our synesthetes put it: 'I have never been able to understand how people can enjoy looking at bloodthirsty films, or laugh at the painful misfortunes of others when I can not only see it but also feel it.' However, this type of synesthesia could also be advantageous. It could make people more caring and empathic. In order to explore this, we needed to find more synesthetes and we soon discovered that this type of synesthesia was more common than we first thought. We managed to find eight more mirror-touch synesthetes from among our existing database of synesthetes. They had never mentioned it to us before because they thought it was 'normal', i.e. they assumed that everyone had it. We also found four more from within the undergraduate population after distributing questionnaires to around 300 people. This means that there are potentially enough people in the UK with this type of synesthesia to fill Liverpool or Edinburgh. One interesting characteristic of this type of synesthesia is that there appear to be two spatial mappings in operation in different people. For some people the spatial mapping is like looking in a mirror, so an observed touch on someone's left cheek would be felt on their right cheek (as if the seen person is a mirror reflection of themselves). For others the mapping is anatomical, such that an observed touch on a left cheek would be experienced on their left cheek (as if the seen person is rotated into their own body, or vice versa).

In order to show that these new synesthetes were genuine, we devised a new task. Participants received small taps on their cheeks and at the same time they watched someone else being touched. They had to say where they were being touched and ignore where the other person had been touched. The synesthetes, but not a group of controls, tended to mistake other people's touch for their own touch.

The mirror-touch synesthetes were given a standard questionnaire that measures empathy. They scored significantly higher on the 'emotional reactivity' component, which relates to their instinctive, gut reaction to others. They didn't score any higher on the questions that relate to the cognitive aspects of empathy, i.e. thinking about what other people feel. This suggests, as one might expect, that the concept of empathy can be broken down into different elements. The emotional aspects may be driven by a multisensory 'mirror system' involving vision and touch that is enhanced in this variety of synesthesia. But it isn't enhanced in all types of synesthesia. Other synesthetes who lack this sensory experience (e.g. synesthetes with colored letters) didn't score any higher on the empathy questionnaire. Coming back to the argument set out at the beginning of the chapter, enhanced empathy is probably a direct consequence of the particular sensory experiences (i.e. mirror-touch synesthesia), rather than a general property of synesthesia. Mirror-touch synesthesia can offer a unique window into how the sense of touch relates to non-sensory ideas such as empathy. But it would be misleading to conclude that 'synesthetes are more empathic' or that 'synesthesia exists to enable empathy', because it doesn't apply to synesthesia in general.

The discovery of so-called mirror systems is one of the most exciting developments in the brain sciences in the past 15 years. Mirror systems were not initially discovered via synesthesia, but by observing how individual cells in the brain respond to observing or performing actions. A set of nerve cells were discovered that responded both when watching another animal perform an action (e.g. grasping or tearing) and when the animal performed the same action itself. That is, these cells in the brain didn't really care whether the action was performed by self or other. Perhaps we comprehend the actions of other people by internally simulating or 'mirroring' their actions in our own brains. These mirror systems are multisensory because they will also respond to the sounds of actions (e.g. a tearing sound). It has been suggested that the system could be defective in autistic people, and it has been suggested that mirror systems may account for language evolution (I will return to this point later).

Mirror systems not only exist for actions but are also found for emotions. If someone else pulls an expression of disgust, then the part of our brain that signals our disgust becomes active. Emotions really are contagious. Smile, and the world smiles with you. Look disgusted, and we will share in your disgust. Mirror systems also exist for different senses. The mirror system for touch was discovered, at least in part, via synesthesia. The mirror system for pain had already been noted prior to touch. There are synesthetes who are the equivalent of 'mirror touch' in other senses, but they have yet to be studied in detail. This includes 'mirror smell', 'mirror taste' and 'mirror hearing'. These different systems are probably independent of each other. It is possible to have mirror touch without mirror taste, and so on. Richard Cytowic was the first to report a synesthete who could smell observed objects (mirror-smell synesthesia). Thus, television commercials for bleach and cookery programs produce a literal kind of smelly-vision. Anne, who has the name that looks like Spanish pimento olives, also sometimes experiences mirror taste. She describes a recent shopping trip:

When I was shopping for whiskey at Christmas I was staring at shelves full of different whiskeys at eye level for several minutes while trying to decide which to choose. As I continued to stare, I had the experience of beginning to taste the whiskey on my tongue and in my head. It surprised me when I realized that I was looking at it and beginning to taste it as well, not just the memory of it but the actual taste.

Mirror systems in general, and these types of synesthesia in particular, bring home the notion of how our world –

even our social world – is constructed from information from the different senses. A strawberry has a color, shape, smell, and taste. But if we encounter only one aspect of it (e.g. the sight of it), then our brain fills in the missing pieces of the multisensory jigsaw. If we see touch or pain, our brain simulates what that touch or pain might feel like even if, for most people, we don't consciously experience the sensation.

Why does synesthesia exist?

Reproduction generates a large amount of genetic variability. Occasionally, a gene may be altered to exist in a nonstandard form. According to evolutionary theory, if this gene is of benefit to the survival of the species then it will become more common in the population because the people who carry the gene will have some relative advantage (e.g. they will be stronger or smarter than people who lack the gene). According to recent prevalence estimates, synesthesia is relatively common; we are all likely to know several people who have it. But what was the evolutionary drive that ensured that it survived within the gene pool?

First of all, it is important to distinguish between the advantages of normal multisensory perception (which are well documented) and any advantages associated with the curious but uncommon form of multisensory perception known as synesthesia. In normal multisensory perception, two senses might be directly stimulated together (e.g. sound and vision) and the information might be combined such that the whole is greater than the sum of the parts. For example, sounds that cannot normally be heard may become audible in the presence of vision. Combining information from different senses may also enable us to locate objects in space by cross-referencing the seen position on the eyes with the felt orientations of our head, hands, and so on. In synesthesia, only one thing (e.g. hearing) is directly stimulated and this indirectly activates a second sense (e.g. vision). Given that the secondary sense is effectively illusory it cannot provide any more additional information about the world than the first sense alone. Whatever the advantages of synesthesia are, they are likely to be distinct from the advantages associated with normal multisensory perception.

One possibility is that synesthesia does not have a function or it did not evolve because it was initially advantageous. There are many conditions with genetic components that are relatively common but are not generally considered to be advantageous (e.g. autism, dyslexia). Certain biological conditions can even be a net disadvantage but still exist in the gene pool. Certain types of cancer have genetic components but they don't get selected out of the gene pool because, for instance, the cancer does not occur until after child-bearing age. Just because something exists in the gene pool doesn't necessarily make it advantageous, and this point is often misunderstood. Synesthesia could be considered to be a benign variation that is neither advantageous nor disadvantageous in evolutionary terms. This is what scientists would term their null hypothesis. Science cannot prove a negative (i.e. that synesthesia lacks a function), but it would be reasonable to draw this conclusion if other lines of enquiry prove fruitless.

What are the candidates for explaining why synesthesia exists that would lead us to discount the null hypothesis? Three serious candidates will be considered here. The first two were proposed primarily by V.S. Ramachandran and Ed Hubbard of the University of California, San Diego; namely, creativity and language evolution. The third I would like to add myself; namely, memory.

The argument from creativity

The argument from creativity really has two separate strands, and I shall consider them separately. The first claim is that synesthesia might be more common in artists, poets, musicians and so on; that is, in people who we assume from first principles to be creative. The second claim is that synesthesia might encourage the development of novel and adaptive ideas. Ramachandran and Hubbard sum up this claim as follows:

Synesthesia causes excess communication amongst brain maps
. . . Depending on where and how widely in the brain the trait
was expressed, it could lead to both synesthesia and to a
propensity toward linking seemingly unrelated concepts and
ideas – in short, creativity. This would explain why the apparently useless synesthesia gene has survived in the population.

The reason I consider these to be separate issues is that I
don't accept that people with artistic inclinations are necessarily more creative than, say, a successful entrepreneur
who has established his/her own business or a research
scientist who is developing new treatments for cancer. The
reasons that some people channel their creative energies
into art and others into business or science are interesting,
but we shouldn't confuse this with whether someone has
more or less creativity as a kind of general mental capacity.
On the face of it, one could imagine that generating novel
ideas and solutions (the second claim) could promote
survival of a gene within a population, but it is unclear
whether a tendency to paint pretty pictures (the first claim)
has survival value against the ravages of war, famine, etc.
The paintbrush may not be mightier than the sword, but
there is evidence that our artistic friends are having more
sex than the rest of us (and thus promoting their genes). A
recent study shows that the amount of time spent on visual
art or poetry predicts the number of sexual partners that a
person has had. This occurs independently of other factors
(e.g. personality traits) that are known to be important. So
both claims about synesthesia and creativity deserve to be
taken seriously.

There are several high-profile artists who may have had
synesthesia, and plenty more who have taken the idea of
synesthesia as an inspiration. Distinguishing between 'true'
and 'inspired-by' synesthesia isn't always possible, especially if the person is dead. In the late nineteenth and early
twentieth centuries, the use of synesthesia (broadly defined)
in art was all the rage. James McNeill Whistler, although
not a synesthete, was interested in creating paintings that
captured aspects of music. His works had titles such as
Nocturne in Black and *Symphony in White*. Wassily

Kandinsky, possibly a synesthete himself, explicitly set out to capture music through a more abstract style of painting. On attending a performance of Wagner, he remarked: 'I saw all my colors in spirit, before my eyes. Wild, almost crazy lines were sketched in front of me.' For Kandinsky, 'music is the best teacher . . . Music has been the art which has devoted itself not to reproduction of natural phenomena, but to the expression of the artist's soul.' Richard Cytowic describes an interview with the British artist, David Hockney, in which Hockney claimed to visualize the colors of the music in order to paint a set for the Metropolitan Opera. Composers, as well as visual artists, may utilize their synesthesia in order to inspire and inform their music. The composer Olivier Messiaen, a likely synesthete, describes how his choice of musical chords may be affected by their color, and his hand-written scores contain many examples in which he has noted down color correspondences. George Gershwin, although not a synesthete himself, chose the title *Rhapsody in Blue* after his brother, Ira, told him about Whistler's approach of giving paintings musical names (the piece was originally destined to be called *American Rhapsody*). Gershwin was effectively doing the opposite of Whistler, naming music after color.

There are a number of contemporary artists whom I have come to know personally and who rely extensively on their synesthesia. Jane Mackay draws inspiration from her synesthetic visions that are triggered by music. These visions constantly evolve in time and space as the music itself unfolds. Putting this on to two-dimensional canvas is not a literal 'paint what you see', as it involves selecting and blending components from the piece and perhaps adding non-synesthetic elements that create the right balance. Philippa Stanton has similar experiences to Jane, but she is a portrait artist. She paints the *voices* of famous people, rather than their faces! This is, as far as I know, an entirely novel concept and it owes its existence to Philippa's synesthesia.

The fact that synesthesia can be fruitfully used in art is well and good, but what about the evolutionary question? Does synesthesia exist to enable art? Why would evolution favour art over other skills more directly related to survival? Lists of famous or contemporary artists who have synesthesia shed no light on whether synesthesia and art go hand in hand. In order to determine this, we need to examine large groups of synesthetes. The survey of Australian synesthetes mentioned above showed that 24 percent were employed in artistic professions compared to a national average of 2 percent. Moreover, they were significantly more likely to be engaged in art (drawing, painting) as a hobby. I have recently conducted a similar survey of synesthetes, mainly based in the UK, showing the same trend. However, I also contrasted different types of synesthesia. Would someone like James Wannerton, whose synesthesia involves taste, be more artistic? Or would it matter if music was a potent trigger of synesthesia? We found that the artistic and musical inclination was strongly influenced by one subtype of synesthesia – visualized music. In terms of playing a musical instrument, there is a strong bias for those who experience complex visions from music to be musical but the trend is not found in any other type of synesthesia. In terms of drawing and painting, this group also shows a very strong tendency, although there is a weaker tendency in other types of synesthesia.

Thus, the problem with the 'synesthesia exists to enable art' idea is that most types of synesthesia have little or no bearing on art. To pursue this argument, one needs to argue that one uncommon type of synesthesia (visualized music) is sufficient to drive the evolutionary process and all the other subtypes are functionless by-products. A more likely scenario, in my view, is that the experiences associated with visualized music are sufficiently rich and beautiful in themselves to provide a powerful source of inspiration to produce art and music. Together with a professional animator, Samantha Moore, we have recently produced animated clips of these synesthetic experiences that have moving textures and shapes that swirl and pulse in time with the rhythm. When we show these animations to people who don't have synesthesia, they judge them to be more aesthetically pleasing than comparable animations from non-synesthetes or even the original synesthetic animation that has been rotated through 90 degrees. This shows that the sound–vision associations of synesthetes have an intrinsic appeal not only to themselves but to others too. It is hardly surprising that these synesthetes have strong interests in music and art. But does it explain why synesthesia, in general, exists? I suggest not.

The real core idea of creativity doesn't concern art. It concerns the development of novel ideas that are useful or meaningful in some way. It concerns flexible thought and thinking outside the box. So let me turn to this particular issue. Psychologists who study creativity have developed a number of different tests that tap some aspect of this process. It enables creativity to be quantified so that we can ask whether one group of people score higher than another. We gave two of these tests to a sample of 82 people with various kinds of synesthesia, and a group of people who don't have it. The first test, called the Remote Associates Test, taps the ability for people to notice disparate but meaningful associations between groups of words. For example, what word links 'stalk, king, trainer'? What word links 'sandwich, golf, foot'? (Answers can be found in the footnote).[1] For the second test, called the Alternate Uses Test, we presented participants with a named object, such as a 'newspaper', and asked them to think of as many uses, aside from reading it, as possible in a short period of time. Common answers include 'start a fire', 'wrap garbage' or 'swat flies'. Less common, but equally correct, answers include 'line drawers' or 'make up a kidnap note'. What did we find? First of all, performance on these tests was unrelated to the amount of time that synesthetes or controls spent in artistic activities. This supports the earlier argument that artistic people are not necessarily more creative. But did synesthetes outperform controls overall? On one of the tests, the Remote Associates, they did. Moreover, their performance was related to the number of types of synesthesia that they possessed (more types of

---

1 The answers are 'lion' and 'club' respectively. These are practice items, rather than real items used in the test.

synesthesia was associated with a higher score) but not the specific type of synesthesia (e.g. taste, color, space) or factors such as age, sex, and education. This finding is clearly within the spirit of the claims made by Ramachandran and Hubbard. The results also get round the thorny problem of whether synesthesia in general has a benefit, or whether it is particular subtypes of synesthesia that are beneficial. Having more types of synesthesia seems to be associated with better performance on the task, irrespective of what the actual types of synesthesia are.

The other test of creativity that we used, Alternate Uses, throws a potential spanner in the works of this theory. There was no benefit of having synesthesia for performing this task. This test, more than the other, can claim to be testing thinking outside the box. The Remote Associates Test is more like thinking inside the box (i.e. thinking of an answer within our current knowledge base). Perhaps synesthetes, because of their unusual sensations, are better able to link existing ideas together. However, there is no evidence at present that they are better able to use these associations in a flexible way to generate novel solutions – this being the hallmark of creativity.

Of course, I am not denying that some synesthetes are creative and that some people use their synesthesia in creative ways. The issue that needs to be addressed is: would they still be creative if they didn't have synesthesia? My feeling is that synesthesia brings certain ideas to the fore. For example, the notion that time and number have a spatial component, and the idea that musical notes can imply size and shape, may be more apparent to someone with synesthesia. But whether these ideas are used creatively or whether the associations 'are what they are' depends on factors unrelated to synesthesia.

The argument from language evolution

The starting point for this argument is the common assumption that words are arbitrary with respect to the idea that they denote. We call it a 'rose', the Spanish call it a 'rosa' and the Greeks call it a 'triantafulla'. But none of this really

Figure 9 Which of these shapes should be called 'Bouba' and which 'Kiki'? Most people think that the rounded shape should be called 'Bouba'. Figure adapted from Ramachandran and Hubbard (2001b).

matters, because a rose is still a rose. The idea of a rose is the same across languages, or as Shakespeare put it in *Romeo and Juliet*: 'What's in a name? That which we call a rose by any other name would smell as sweet.' But has language always been like this? And is language really like this now? One audacious claim is that the sounds of words (and the lip movements that produce them) often bear a meaningful relationship with the idea that the word denotes. According to many contemporary researchers, these mappings could have enabled language evolution itself to have taken root. Ideas could be more easily transferred from one person's head into another's (via language) if the sounds themselves were meaningfully related to the ideas being conveyed. Where would such meaningful mappings between the senses come from? I'll give you one guess.

Consider the famous example given by Ramachandran and Hubbard which is based on the research of Wolfgang Köhler in the 1920s. Look at the shapes in Figure 9 and tell me which is called 'Bouba' and which is called 'Kiki'. If you behaved like almost 100 percent of the population, then you would say that 'Bouba' was the name of the rounded shape and 'Kiki' was the name of the spiky shape. Now imagine that you are a grunting pre-linguistic *homo sapiens* living 30 to one hundred thousand years ago. You come across two plants, one with rounded leaves and the other with spiky leaves and you want to warn your tribe members that the round-leaved plant is poisonous. How would you convey that information? The idea of poison could perhaps be conveyed by a look of facial disgust with a wrinkling of the nose. But perhaps a vocalization such as an 'urrrgh' sound could be used instead because the production of this sound mimics some of the facial gestures of disgust. Similarly, the concept of roundness could be conveyed by hand gestures; an early form of sign language maybe. Or perhaps it could be conveyed by a roundness of the lips and smooth (rather than abrupt) sound modulations by producing a 'bouba'-like grunt. This, in essence, is the argument that has been put forward for a link between synesthesia and language evolution.

Before considering the evidence for and against this argument, it is important to rule out one trivial explanation of the Bouba/Kiki finding, namely that it is due to the shape of the letters 'B' and 'K'. The basic result has been replicated in two illiterate populations (albeit using slightly different words and shapes). The first was in the 1960s in a tribe in Tanganyika (now Tanzania), and the second was performed recently in Canadian preschool children prior to their being taught how to read or write. Both groups could match Bouba/round and Kiki/angular despite having no literacy. So what is it that gives rise to such remarkably high consistency between people? At present it is unclear. One idea is that it is related to the sound of the consonants, such that consonants with abrupt onsets (e.g. 'k') are more likely to be judged angular. Another idea is that it could relate to the mouth shape in producing the vowels. An 'oo' sound (as in 'boot') has rounded lips, but an 'ee' sound (as in 'eel') does not.

One of the most popular contemporary accounts of the evolution of language is that language evolved from hand gestures. So-called mirror systems in the brain respond both when watching other animals performing actions and when producing actions themselves. These mirror systems may enable us to understand the actions of others by internally mimicking their actions. Obviously, we don't literally echo back the action of others in terms of copying everything they do, but our brains simulate what the action might feel like and what the goal of the action could be. The evolutionary transition between our primate ancestors and modern humans could be that this mirror system has moved away from hand actions to lip and vocal tract gestures; in short, from signing to speaking. Remnants of a hand-based gestural foundation of language may remain in us today. It is very hard not to gesticulate when speaking, even when on the telephone. In this instance, no-one, except possibly the speaker, could benefit from the gestures. Sign language in the deaf is obviously a pure gesture-based language, and it is indeed a language with its own grammar and other rules. Interestingly, many of the gestures are not arbitrary but are partly related to the meaning of the word. Thus, the sign for 'hammer' involves a downward hand motion and the sign for 'give' involves a forward hand motion.

Perhaps such trends were transferred from hand movements to lip movements. Several scientists claim that the earliest spoken language would have been largely composed of the oral equivalents of these meaningful gestures, guided by some of the rules that we have seen applied in synesthesia. Maybe the earliest words for 'give' were associated with an outward expulsion of air, and 'take' associated with an inward breath. In synesthetes, I have already noted that high-pitched noises tend to elicit smaller visual experiences (Chapter 3) and non-synesthetes show evidence of the same trend, for example when asked to judge size and ignore an irrelevant sound. Perhaps high-pitched vowels were used to denote small concepts in the earliest languages. The strength of this evolutionary theory (like so many others) is that it cannot be disproven. For a scientific theory, this is also its weakness. We cannot go back in time and observe the transition from grunts and hand gestures to speech. We can, however, look for these trends in modern languages. We can also give modern-day speakers artificial words to learn (as in Bouba/Kiki) in order to see which ideas are most readily associated with them. A summary of some of these studies will suffice for the present discussion.

- If people are told that two invented words 'mal' and 'mil' refer to tables and are asked which table is smaller, most people chose the higher pitched vowel ('mil').

- One summary of diverse languages found that the high-pitched vowel 'i' (in 'kid') tended to predominate in words denoting children, small animals, etc.
- Male and female names have different sound patterns. Male names are likely to have fewer syllables and have stress on the first syllable, whereas female names are more likely to contain the 'i' (in Lisa, Celia) and end in a vowel sound.
- English-speaking people can classify names of birds and fishes in Huambisa (a language of north central Peru) more accurately than expected by chance, suggesting that the assignment of words to concepts is not arbitrary.

The evidence discussed above is fascinating. But none of these studies are directly concerned with synesthesia. The problem is that virtually everyone is capable of associating 'Bouba' with a round shape even if they lack synesthesia, so what is the added value of having synesthesia? I have already noted that it is important to separate out the advantages of normal multisensory perception from any advantages of synesthesia. It is possible that multisensory perception has benefits that extend beyond the senses, into other realms such as language. There is tantalizing evidence that it does. However, in order to make a claim about synesthesia (present in the few), rather than multisensory perception (present in everyone), one would need to establish that people with synesthesia are better at making these kinds of correspondences. Only then would we have an explanation as to why synesthesia might be a prized trait that would be favored by evolution. Unfortunately, there is no such evidence. At present, the argument from language evolution does not strike me as a credible explanation for why synesthesia exists. The importance of multisensory links in language evolution remains a possibility.

The argument from superior memory

In the previous chapter, I discussed two synesthetes with extraordinary memories: Daniel Tammet and Solomon Shereshevskii. However, both Tammet and Shereshevskii were extraordinary in other ways. One had autism and an unusual fascination with numbers, and the other had extensively trained his memory. This makes it impossible to be certain how much of their ability is attributable to synesthesia. In order to ascertain this, we would need to look at a wider sample of synesthetes.

It is quite straightforward to imagine how a superior memory would convey an evolutionary advantage, even if the memory was superior only in particular domains (e.g. words, sequences, and numbers). We started by circulating a questionnaire to 46 synesthetes and 46 controls with a similar range of ages (given that memory declines in later life). The synesthetes were far more likely to rate their memory as 'better than average' and they were more likely to report visual strategies for remembering a telephone number (e.g. taking a mental picture, remembering a sequence of colors). Some of these synesthetes were then selected to take part in laboratory tests of memory to see if their memory really was better than average. The synesthetes were better at learning and remembering lists of words than controls. All synesthetes tested experienced colors for words. Interestingly, the synesthetes also had a better memory for color. They were better able to recall the position of colored squares placed in a grid. They could also remember very precise hues using stimuli that are similar to the color swatches used for decorating. However, in other tests they did not outperform the control group, which suggests that their memory is not globally superior. For instance, they were no better than controls when they had to memorize a complex figure that is hard to verbalize.

Case studies of other synesthetes are also consistent with our findings. The synesthetes outperform controls when given verbal material that elicits synesthesia (e.g. numbers or people's names), but not when given material unrelated to their synesthesia. One other feature of synesthetic memory is noteworthy. In many of these tests, the synesthetes were only superior to other people in terms of their ability to retain information rather than the initial speed with which they learn. Synesthetes, apparently, find it harder to forget. One of the reasons why this is interesting is that it differs from individuals who have superior memory because they have extensively trained their memory using mnemonic techniques. People trained in using deliberate memory strategies tend to be able to remember a large volume of information in a short space of time, but the information is easily forgotten. John Wilding and Elizabeth Valentine provide an excellent overview of superior memory ability, contrasting 'naturals' with 'strategists'. One of their conclusions is that 'superior retention is the single most significant characteristic of a naturally superior memory'. The same appears to be true of the natural memory ability of synesthetes.

Why does synesthesia give a natural memory advantage? The answer seems simple. Storing a memory using a variety of codes – verbal, sensory, and spatial – is better than using one code. The same is true of normal memory. If people are given lists of pictures to remember and some items on the list are accompanied by a beep (making them multisensory), these are subsequently better remembered. It just so happens that synesthetes are able to do this by virtue of their unusual sensory experiences. The same is probably true for most, if not all varieties of synesthesia, although all existing research has been done on color. There is probably another reason why their memory is so good: synesthetes who experience colors from letters and words have better memory for colors, as well as better memories for words, even though colors don't trigger additional experiences. Their color system is likely to be finely tuned and more robust to the effects of forgetting than the color system of non-synesthetes.

It is to be noted that, in this account, the evolutionary importance of synesthesia is intimately tied to the synesthetic experiences themselves. The benefits to memory are a direct consequence of the altered sensory experiences and are not a by-product, a colorful sideshow, of other differences in synesthetic brains.

I think it is too early to give a definitive answer to the question: why does synesthesia exist? However, it would be unfair of me to leave the question wide open. We have made some progress. The idea that language could have evolved on the back of multisensory associations is attractive, but these associations are present in people who lack synesthesia and so I don't think it is likely that synesthesia exists because it contributed to language evolution. Nor do I think that synesthesia exists to promote art. An artistic inclination appears to be primarily associated with one particular subtype of synesthesia, visualized music. The same is true of enhanced empathy and mirror-touch synesthesia. The argument from creativity is seductive and I wouldn't like to rule it out completely. Synesthetes do appear to score higher on at least one measure of creativity (word associations) but not necessarily on thinking outside the box. However, if I were a gambling man then my money would be on memory. In this account, the sensory experiences that define synesthesia are directly related to their wider evolutionary function.

Vive la difference

Whatever synesthesia means in the grand scheme of things, it is just an integral part of the daily lives of people who have it. Returning to this theme seems like a fitting conclusion to the book. Although science seeks to study synesthesia objectively, we will only get a full picture of what synesthesia is by embedding the science in the lives of the people who have it.

What does having synesthesia mean to you? What do you think it must be like for other people who do not have synesthesia? I put these questions to some of the people whom I have quoted throughout this book.

Zanna believes that: 'On a day-to-day basis, having synesthesia means very little – most of the time I forget that I'm even doing it. However, I find it fascinating and enjoy helping with research studies into it.' Daniel Tammet also feels that scientific investigations into his synesthesia (and his autism) are important for understanding his world. As he puts it: 'I feel grateful for living now and not half a century ago.' Others, such as Rolf, feel that synesthesia has influenced some of the key decisions that they have made in life:

I think that making an early decision to be an artist is entirely due to my 'unusual' perception of things – though I did not know this at the time. Often I wish I wasn't so distracted by it, as it is intrusive, and frequently makes me daydream! I can't imagine what it would be like to lose it – maybe like losing an eye and having to cope without stereo vision.

Not only are the experiences of synesthetes baffling to those who don't have synesthesia; the reverse is also true. As Rosemary puts it:

Family members are baffled by my synesthesia and I am equally baffled as to how their inner mental world works. Are their thought processes monochrome? Do they not even have a mental picture of words and sentences spelt out as they talk or listen to speech? How do they deal with time and dates? For example, how would they 'picture' a forthcoming date or 'look' back in time when working out what they did the weekend before last? Or view their date of birth, or think back to an earlier century?

Whatever else synesthesia tells us, it tells us that our own way of sensing the world is precious even if we don't literally look back on time, taste runny eggs when reading about New York, or hear blue-croaking frogs.

Notes

Chapter 1: The colorful albino

Page 1–2. A historical account of George Sachs is provided in Jewanski and Ward (in preparation). The original dissertation is Sachs (1812) and the later revised German translation is Schlegel (1824). The obituary of Sachs appeared in *National Zeitung der Deutschen* (6 May 1814) and was kindly brought to my attention by Jörg Jewanski.

Aliens in the family

Page 3. Steen (2001).

Page 7. Barnett *et al.* (in press) show that related synesthetes have no more colors in common than unrelated synesthetes.

Page 7. Rich *et al.* (2005) compared synesthetic colors with colored alphabet books.

Page 7. Ward *et al.* (2005) report that taste synesthetes tend to have relatives with synesthetic color (this being a more common type of synesthesia).

Page 8. Molecular genetic studies of synesthesia: Dublin, Ireland (www.tcd.ie/Psychology/synres); Texas, USA (www.synesthete.org).

Page 8. Discordant sets of identical twins (Smilek *et al.*, 2006, 2005).

Page 9. Sean Day's list of types of synesthesia can be found in Day (2005) and online at http://home.comcast.net/~sean.day/html/types.htm

Page 9. Steen (2001).

Page 10. Human social group sizes of 150 (Dunbar, 1992).

Page 10–11. The prevalence of synesthesia (Sagiv *et al.*, 2006; Simner *et al.*, 2006).

Page 11. The quotes from famous synesthetes come from Nabokov (1967), Feynman, (1988) and Wittgenstein (*Zettel* 185, 32e).

The rise and fall of synesthesia

Page 12. Goethe (1810, based on English translation of 1982).

Page 12. Color illusions including the USA flag after-image can be found at www.planetperplex.com/en/optical_illusions.html

Page 13. The 1814 encyclopedia reference is cited in Dann (1998).

Page 13. Cornaz (1848). The subsequent new cases of synesthesia were two cases in Wartmann (1849) and a case in an anonymous article in *Openheims Zeitschrift* (1849).

Page 13. Krohn (1892) gives a summary of synesthesia in the 1860s and 1870s. Kaiser (1872) and Stevens (1892) offered psychological accounts whereas physiological accounts were offered by Perroud (1863), Chabalier (1864), Lussana (1873), and others.

Page 14. Bleuler and Lehmann (1881).

Page 14. Galton gives his most extensive account of synesthesia in Galton (1883). It is available online at www.fullbooks.com/ Inquiries-into-Human-Faculty-and-Its.html. The quote is taken from Galton (1880).

Page 14–15. Calkins (1895). For biographical information see www.webster.edu/~woolflm/marycalkins.html

Page 15. Simon O'Sullivan (2006) has traced the etymology of the word 'synesthesia'.

Page 16. Howells (1944) is an example of a behaviorist approach to synesthesia.

Can a blind man hear scarlet?

Page 16–19. The account of Molyneux's question and the quotes from Cheselden and Diderot were taken from Morgan (1977). The case of Sydney Bradford was reported by Gregory and Wallace (1963).

Page 17. The description of Thomas Cutsforth is taken from Wheeler and Cutsforth (1921a, 1921b).

Page 19. Hull (1990).

Page 20. Brain imaging has shown that when blind people read Braille, the parts of the brain normally dedicated to vision become activated (Sadato *et al.*, 1996). The same happens when blind people are required to determine where in the room a sound is located (Weeks *et al.*, 2000).

Page 20. Rao *et al.* (2007) give an account of acquired synesthesia following blindness.

Page 21. The blindfolding study is by Merabet *et al.* (2004).

Page 21–2 The accounts of LSD and mescaline are taken from Hofmann (1980, www.hallucinogens.com/hofmann/index.html), Krill *et al.* (1963) and Huxley (1954).

Page 22–3. The sound-to-vision sensory substitution system is described in www.seeingwithsound.com, including a down-loaded (23 May 2007) interview with Pat Fletcher. A scientific account is given in Amedi *et al.* (2007). The touch-to-vision sensory substitution system is discussed in Bach-y-Rita (1972). A recent study has shown that stimulation of the 'visual' cortex in blind people trained to use a tongue-based touch-to-vision sensory substitution system evokes tactile (not visual) sensations (Kupers *et al.*, 2006).

Page 23. The early pioneers of synesthesia research had speculated on the existence of a 'chromatic center'. This is mentioned in Krohn (1892) and attributed to Lussana (1873) and Baratoux. The following quote (from Krohn) is conceptually very modern: 'In 1875, Lussana wrote that the sensorial centers of sound and color in the human brain could be contiguous and thus influence each other in perceiving.'

Page 23–4. Area V4 and cerebral achromatopsia (Zeki, 1993).

Page 25. The case of Jonathan I. is taken from Sacks (1995) and is also discussed in Ione and Tyler (2004).

Not enough points on the chicken

Page 26. The chicken anecdote is taken from Cytowic (1993). The original scientific account was published by Cytowic and Wood (1982).

Page 27. Elizabeth Stewart-Jones was reported in Baron-Cohen *et al.* (1987) and the later study of grapheme–color synesthesia is by Baron-Cohen *et al.* (1993).

Page 28. The brain imaging study is by Nunn *et al.* (2002).

Page 29. The nineteenth-century study of naming times for synesthetic colors is by Beaunis and Binet (1892).

Page 30. The obituary of Sachs appeared in *National Zeitung der Deutschen* (6 May 1814).

Chapter 2: Counting on the senses

Page 31–2. The *New Scientist* article appeared on 29 January 2005, by B. Durie ('Senses special: Doors of perception'). Charles Spence brought the article, and the question of how many sense we have, to my attention. Keeley (2002) provides an interesting philosophical perspective on how human and animal senses can be individuated. The bread-smelling-garlic example was adapted from http://plato.stanford.edu/entries/aristotle-psychology/#6

Page 32. Kensinger (1995) describes the Cashinahua senses.

Page 34. The disembodied woman (Sacks, 1985).

Page 34. Craig (2002) provides a review of interoception and includes pain and thermal sensations as part of interoception.

Page 34. Colored pain described by Dudycha and Dudycha (1935).

The buzzing world of babies

Page 36. 'Blooming, buzzing confusion' (James, 1890).

Page 37. Maurer and Maurer (1988). See also Maurer and Mondloch (2006) for the most recent arguments.

Page 37–8. EEG studies of infants: sound–touch (Wolff *et al.*, 1974), sound–vision (Neville, 1995).

Page 38. Lewkowicz and Turkewitz (1980).

Page 39. Dummy/pacifier study (Meltzoff and Borton, 1979) and the tactile–visual square/star study (Streri, 1987).

Page 39. 'Studies of the brain anatomy in other species . . .' (Dehay *et al.*, 1984; Innocenti and Clarke, 1984).

Page 40. Early tuning-in to the phonemes of our language (Eimas, 1975).

Page 41. Verhagen and Engelen (2006) suggest that taste–smell may fail to differentiate out from an early unitary synesthetic sense because experience keeps them together. Stevenson and

Tomiczek (2007) provide a recent review suggesting that smell–taste is a universal type of synesthesia.

Page 41. Adding a sweet-smelling odor to a sweet-tasting liquid makes the liquid 'taste' sweeter (Frank and Byram, 1988).

Page 41. People who have lost their sense of taste also lose the ability to categorize smells in terms of taste properties (Stevenson *et al.*, in press).

Page 41. Vietnamese smell–taste pairings differ from those in the West (Chrea *et al.*, 2004).

Page 41. An unfamiliar odor that is initially judged not to smell 'sweet', 'sour', or 'bitter' can acquire these labels very rapidly (Yeomans *et al.*, 2006) and is very robust to unlearning (Stevenson *et al.*, 2000).

Page 42. Some people retain the synesthesia of their infancy into adulthood (Baron-Cohen, 1996; Maurer, 1997).

Page 42–5. Studies of James Wannerton (Ward and Simner, 2003; Ward *et al.*, 2005).

When sound and vision collide

Page 46–7. Colliding versus passing bars (Bushara *et al.*, 2003).

Page 47. Double flash illusion (Shams *et al.*, 2000, 2001).

Page 48. The McGurk illusion (McGurk and MacDonald, 1976).

Page 49. An account of Müller's doctrine is given by Finger and Wade (2002).

Page 49. Multisensory integration in neurons (e.g. Stein *et al.*, 1988).

Page 50. The ventriloquist illusion (e.g. Driver, 1996).

Page 50–1. Dalton *et al.* (2000) describe olfactory enhancement by integration of subthreshold taste and smell. Sumby and Pollack (1954) conducted a similar study with heard and seen speech.

Page 51. Perceived hand dryness affected by auditory feedback (Guest *et al.*, 2002).

Page 51. Perceived smoothness of toothbrushes (Zampini *et al.*, 2003).

Page 51. A picture feels like it is displayed longer (Vroomen and de Gelder, 2000) and is judged to be brighter when it is accompanied by a sound (Stein *et al.*, 1996), and sound is judged to be louder when accompanied by bright vision (Odgaard *et al.*, 2004).

Page 51. Tactile perception improved by observing the body part (Kennett *et al.*, 2001).

From blind dinners to The Fat Duck

Page 52. www.danslenoir.com

Page 54. www.fatduck.co.uk

Page 56. Evolution of color vision (Mollon, 1991).

Page 57. Even expert wine tasters can be thrown by the color (Morrot *et al.*, 2001).

Page 57. Accuracy at identifying the odor of solutions is related to color (Zellner *et al.*, 1991) and odors presented in colored solutions smell stronger (Zellner and Kautz, 1990).

Page 57. Increased thickness reduces perceived odor intensity (Hollowood *et al.*, 2002).

Page 57. Auditory amplification of sparkling water (Zampini and Spence, 2005) and Pringles chips (Zampini and Spence, 2004).

Page 57. Kellogg's attempted to patent the sound of their cornflakes (Lindstrom, 2005).

Chapter 3: An altered reality

Page 59. Duffy (2001)

Page 60. Synesthetes tend to see high-pitched sounds as being smaller and lighter in color (Marks, 1975).

Crossing the Rubicon: from multisensory perception to synesthesia

Page 60. Crossing the Rubicon. The phrase relates to Julius Caesar who crossed the river Rubicon with his army in 49 BC and had effectively instigated a point of no return in his military campaign.

Page 62. Other species have multisensory perception (see Stein and Meredith, 1993).

Page 63. Synesthetes are more likely to be artistic (Rich *et al.*, 2005).

Page 63. Rich *et al.* (2005) compared synesthetes' colored letters with colored alphabet books. A few synesthetes have been shown to have been influenced by these (Hancock, 2006; Witthoft and Winawer, 2006).

Page 63–4. Ramachandran and Hubbard (2001a, 2001b) suggest that adjacency may determine the types of synesthesia that are naturally observed.

Page 64. Ward and Sagiv (2007) report synesthesia for dice patterns and finger counting.

Page 65. Ward *et al.* (2005) compared seven taste synesthetes with seven color synesthetes.

Page 66. The personification of letters and numbers is reported in Simner and Holenstein (2007) and Smilek *et al.* (2007). The two quotes are taken, respectively, from these publications.

Page 67. Duffy (2001).

Page 67. Mills *et al.* (2002).

Page 68. Ward *et al.* (2006a), colored musical notation.

Page 68. Braille reading uses the same brain regions as visual reading (Büchel *et al.*, 1998).

Page 69. The onset of the synesthesia didn't coincide with the onset of the blindness by months or years (case 8, Jacobs *et al.*, 1981; Rao *et al.*, 2007) but in other cases the synesthesia occurred within one to three days after onset of blindness (Jacobs *et al.*, 1981).

Page 69. Visual experiences after blindfolding (Merabet *et al.*, 2004).

Page 70. Involvement of the CIA in LSD experimentation (Lee and Shlain, 1985).

Page 70. Eleusinian mysteries (Wasson *et al.*, 1978).

Page 70. The Harvard professor, Timothy Leary, who championed the psychedelic movement took a different approach to the psychologists of the day – 'We would avoid the behaviorist approach to others' awareness' (Leary, 1968).

Page 71. Quotes from Stoll and Hofmann are in Hofmann (1980) and a full online version is available at www.hallucinogens.com/hofmann/index.html

Page 72. The visual abilities of people inebriated with these drugs deteriorate (Carlson, 1958; Hartman and Hollister, 1963).

Page 72. Improved color perception in synesthesia (Yaro and Ward, 2007).

Why 'O' is white and Chopin is yellow

Page 73. Simner *et al.* (2005). Patterns in letter–color associations.

Page 75. Color organs (Peacock, 1988).

Page 75. Marks (1975).

Page 75. Pitch–lightness association after taking mescaline (cited in Critchley, 1977).

Page 75–6. Ward *et al.* (2006b). Sound–color synesthesia.

Page 76. Marks (1987). Pitch–lightness interactions affect the speed of judgments in non-synesthetes. Marks (1982a, 1982b): synesthetic metaphor in poetry.

Page 76. Do small white balls squeak? (Mondloch and Maurer, 2004).

Page 76. Even one-month-old infants can match auditory pitch with visual brightness (Lewkowicz and Turkewitz, 1980).

Page 77. Pitch and space in non-synesthetes (Ben-Artzi and Marks, 1995) and infants (Wagner *et al.*, 1981).

Page 77. High pitch is smaller (Gallace and Spence, 2006).

Page 78. Duration and type of instrument affect the synesthetic shape (Zigler, 1930).

Page 78. Number–lightness (Cohen Kadosh and Henik, 2006b).

Page 78. Battig and Montague (1969) report the order of generation of color names.

Page 79. Berlin and Kay (1969). See also Regier, Kay and Khetarpal (2007) for an updated view. Related to frequency of occurrence in natural environments (Yendrikhovskij, 2001).

Page 80. Simner *et al.* (2005). Patterns in letter–color associations.

Page 80. Color associations to X and O in preliterate children (Spector and Maurer, in press).

Page 81. Colors of days of the week (Shanon, 1982).

Can synesthesia be turned off?

Page 82. Jonathan I. (Sacks, 1995).

Page 82. 18% said their synesthesia was enhanced when they were happy and 0% said it was reduced (61% said it didn't make a difference and 21% didn't know). There were 127 respondents.

Page 82. Nose quote from Rich *et al.* (2005).

Page 83. Simons and Chabris (1999).

Page 83–4. Stroop (1935). Wollen and Ruggiero (1983) were the first to attempt a Stroop task of synesthesia.

Page 84. 'It is wrong . . .' quote from Callejas *et al.* (2007).

Page 84–5. The local/global stimulus competition was first reported by Ramachandran and Hubbard (2001b) and systematically explored by Rich and Mattingley (2003).

Page 85–6. Mattingley *et al.* (2006).

Chapter 4: The screen in my forehead

Page 89–91. A popular science account of how space is perceived by the brain is given by Morgan (2003).

Page 91. Map of London Underground based on walking time (rodcorp.typepad.com/rodcorp/2003/10/london_tube_map.html).

The phantom touch

Page 91–2. The case of George Dedlow (Mitchell, 1866): www.pain online.org/Dedlow.htm. Although Dedlow is now recognized as a fictitious case, the author, Silas Weir Mitchell, worked extensively with war amputees and based much of his account on his observations.

Page 92. Ramachandran and Hirstein (1998) provide an excellent summary of phantom limb phenomena.

Page 92. Synesthesia can modify the phantom limb experience (Ramachandran and Rogers-Ramachandran, 1996; Ramachandran *et al.*, 1995).

Page 94–5. The rubber hand illusion was first reported by Botvinick and Cohen (1998). Armel and Ramachandran (2003) show that bending the finger back can produce a sweat response. Gurgin *et al.* (2007) show that a laser pen on the rubber arm can trigger thermal and tactile sensations.

Different types of space

Page 96–7. Colby and Goldberg (1999) offer a good review of coordinate transformations in the brain.

Page 97–8. Different spatial locations of numbers and time. Galton (1883; online at www.fullbooks.com/Inquiries-into-Human-Faculty-and-Its.html) offers several accounts. Ward *et al.* (2007) report a number of different spatial locations. Pat Duffy's calendar form is reported in Smilek *et al.* (2006) and Duffy (2001). Steven and Blakemore (2004) also note different spatial reference frames including head- and body-centered.

Page 98–100. Projector–associator distinction. Dixon *et al.* (2004) report the experiment of naming real versus synesthetic colors. Ward *et al.* (2007) replicate the basic result and show that projectors are more likely to report colors for briefly flashed graphemes (although not necessarily the correct color). They also argue that the projector–associator distinction does not go far enough. The *Lancet* article is Colman (1894). Downey (1911) reports the case of colored taste.

Page 101–2. Auras as a possible type of synesthesia are discussed in Ward (2004). Riggs and Karwoski (1934) describe the case of the seven-year-old. The description of Matilda is based on personal correspondence.

Page 102–3. Acquired types of synesthesia: sound–vision (Jacobs *et al.*, 1981); touch–vision (Armel and Ramachandran, 1999).

A space to think

Page 103. Projecting visual images into external space is called eidetic imagery (Haber, 1979). The prevalence in children is reported by Giray *et al.* (1976).

Page 103–4. Synesthetes have more vivid visual imagery (Barnett and Newell, in press).

Page 104–5. Dehaene *et al.* (1998) provide an overview of their theory. Dehaene *et al.* (1993) report the left–right spatial bias in odd–even judgments.

Page 105. Prevalence of number forms in the synesthetic and general population (Sagiv *et al.*, 2006). Galton (1883) and Piazza *et al.* (2006) describe some unusual number forms. Ward *et al.* (submitted) report multiplication to be slower in synesthetes with number forms.

Page 106. 'Five plus two equals yellow' (Dixon *et al.*, 2000). The colored line study is by Cohen Kadosh and Henik (2006b).

Page 106. Gevers *et al.* (2003) report a left–right spatial bias in responding to months of the year.

The pi man

Page 110. Tammet (2006) and www.optimnem.co.uk

Page 111. Many synesthetes regard languages as a strength (Rich *et al.*, 2005). The same study also shows that synesthetes are not more likely to be left-handed than other individuals.

Page 112. 10% of autistic people have exceptional abilities (Hill and Frith, 2003).

Page 113. Wilding and Valentine (1997) discuss the method of loci and show that memory experts who rely heavily on this and similar strategies have normal memory performance on other tasks.

Page 113. Yaro and Ward (2007) show that synesthetes, but not others, tend to report remembering phone numbers visually.

Page 113. Tammet's memory has 'islands of ability' (based on personal communication, 23 July 2007).

Page 114–16. Luria (1968).

Chapter 5: Beyond the senses

Page 117. Survey of Australian synesthetes (Rich *et al.*, 2005).

Page 118. Tammet (2006) claims algebra is poor. Ward *et al.* (submitted) examined claims of maths problems in synesthesia.

A touching sight

Page 120. Touch definitions from www.answers.com, 10 July 2007.

Page 120. Cultural rules about touch (Classen, 2005). Quote from Clinton (2004).

Page 120–1. Grooming (Keverne *et al.*, 1989).

Page 121. Touch by other people is perceived by the brain as more intense (Blakemore *et al.*, 1998).

Page 121–3. Brain imaging study of mirror-touch synesthesia (Blakemore *et al.*, 2005). Mirror touch and empathy (Banissy and Ward, 2007). A mirror system for touch was independently found by Keysers *et al.* (2004).

Page 123. Recent review of mirror neurons (Rizzolatti *et al.*, 2001). Mirror neurons and the sound of actions (Gazzola *et al.*, 2006); autism (Oberman *et al.*, 2005); and language evolution (Rizzolatti and Arbib, 1998).

Page 124. Perception of disgust (Wicker *et al.*, 2003) and pain (Singer *et al.*, 2004).

Page 124. Cytowic (2002) reports mirror-smell synesthesia (which he calls olfactory memory).

Why does synesthesia exist?

The argument from creativity

Page 127. The quote is from Ramachandran and Hubbard (2003). Ramachandran and Hubbard (2001b) provide the most detailed account of this argument.

Page 127. Artists have more sexual partners (Nettle and Clegg, 2006).

Page 127–8. Brougher *et al.* (2005) is an excellent source for synesthetic influences in art and, to a lesser extent, in music. The accounts of Hockney, Messiaen, and Kandinsky are taken from Cytowic (2002), Bernard (1986), and McDonell (1990) respectively.

Page 128. Philippa Stanton (www.philippastanton.com) and Jane Mackay (www.soundingart.com).

Page 129. Australian survey (Rich *et al.*, 2005) and UK survey (Ward *et al.*, in press b).

Page 129. Ward *et al.* (in press a) describe the animation study with Samantha Moore.

Page 130–1. Ward *et al.* (in press b) investigate the amount of time spent doing art and music as a function of type of synesthesia, and performance on two measures of creativity.

The argument from language evolution

Page 132. Ramachandran and Hubbard (2001b) provide the most detailed account of this argument, including the Bouba/Kiki example.

Page 133. Sound–shape correspondences in Tanzania (Davis, 1961) and preliterate children (Maurer *et al.*, 2006).

Page 133. Bouba/Kiki effect could relate to onset of consonants (e.g. Westbury, 2005) or roundedness of vowels (Maurer *et al.*, 2006).

Page 133–4. The role of mirror systems in language evolution is discussed by Corballis (2002) and Rizzolatti and Arbib (1998).

Page 134–5. Mal/mil (Sapir, 1929); 'i' to denote small things (Jespersen, 1933); male/female names (Cutler *et al.*, 1990); birds and fishes in Huambisa (Berlin, 1994).

The argument from superior memory

Page 136. Yaro and Ward (2007) conducted the survey of synesthetes' memory and the subsequent objective tests of memory.

Page 136–7. Other case studies of memory in synesthetes are reported by Smilek *et al.* (2002a) and Mills *et al.* (2006).

Page 137. Wilding and Valentine (1997).

Page 137. If some items on the list are accompanied by a beep then they are subsequently better remembered (Murray *et al.*, 2004).

References

Amedi, A., Stern, W., Camprodon, J. A., Bermpohl, F., Merabet, L., Rotman, S., Hemond, C., Meijer, P., & Pascual-Leone, A. (2007). Shape conveyed by visual-to-auditory sensory substitution activates the lateral occipital complex. *Nature Neuroscience, 10*, 687–689.

Anonymous. (1849). *Oppenheims Zeitschrift, Band XL* (Heft. 4).

Armel, K. C., & Ramachandran, V. S. (1999). Acquired synaesthesia in retinitis pigmentosa. *Neurocase, 5*, 293–296.

Armel, K. C., & Ramachandran, V. S. (2003). Projecting sensations to external objects: Evidence from skin conductance response. *Proceedings of the Royal Society of London: Biological, 270*, 1499–1506.

Bach-y-Rita, P. (1972). *Brain mechanisms in sensory substitution.* New York: Academic Press.

Banissy, M., & Ward, J. (2007). Mirror touch synaesthesia is linked with empathy. *Nature Neuroscience, 10*, 815–816.

Barnett, K. J., Finucane, C., Asher, J. E., Bargary, G., Corvin, A. P., Newell, F. N., & Mitchell, K. J. (in press). Familial patterns and the origins of individual differences in synaesthesia. *Cognition.*

Barnett, K. J., & Newell, F. N. (in press). Synaesthesia is associated with enhanced, self-rated visual imagery. *Consciousness and Cognition.*

Baron-Cohen, S. (1996). Is there a normal phase of synaesthesia in development? *Psyche, 2*, 27.

Baron-Cohen, S., Harrison, J., Goldstein, L. H., & Wyke, M. (1993). Coloured speech perception: Is synaesthesia what happens when modularity breaks down? *Perception, 22*, 419–426.

Baron-Cohen, S., Wyke, M. A., & Binnie, C. (1987). Hearing words and seeing colours: An experimental investigation of a case of synaesthesia. *Perception, 16*, 761–767.

Battig, W. F., & Montague, W. E. (1969). Category norms for verbal items in 56 categories: A replication and extension of the Connecticut category norms. *Journal of Experimental Psychology Monograph, 80,* 1–45.

Beaunis, H., & Binet, A. (1892). Sur deux cas d'audition colorée. *Revue Philosophique, 33,* 448–461.

Ben-Artzi, E., & Marks, L. E. (1995). Visual–auditory interaction in speeded classification: Role of stimulus difference. *Perception and Psychophysics, 57,* 1151–1162.

Berlin, B. (1994). Evidence for pervasive synesthetic sound symbolism in ethnozoological nomenclature. In L. Hinton, J. Nichols & J. J. Ohala (Eds.), *Sound Symbolism.* Cambridge: Cambridge University Press.

Berlin, B., & Kay, P. (1969). *Basic colour terms: Their universality and evolution.* Berkeley, CA: University of California Press.

Bernard, J. W. (1986). Messiaen's synaesthesia: The correspondence between color and sound structure in his music. *Music Perception, 4,* 41–68.

Blakemore, S.-J., Bristow, D., Bird, G., Frith, C., & Ward, J. (2005). Somatosensory activations during the observation of touch and a case of vision–touch synesthesia. *Brain, 128,* 1571–1583.

Blakemore, S.-J., Rees, G., & Frith, C. D. (1998). How do we predict the consequences of our actions? A functional imaging study. *Neuropsychologia, 36,* 521–529.

Bleuler, E., & Lehmann, K. (1881). *Zwangsmaessige Lichtempfindungen durch Scall, und verwandte Erscheinungen auf dem Gebiete der anderen Sinnesempfindungen.* Leipzig: Fues's Verlag.

Botvinick, M., & Cohen, J. (1998). Rubber hands 'feel' touch that eyes see. *Nature, 391,* 756.

Brougher, K., Strick, J., Wiseman, A., & Zilczer, J. (2005). *Visual music: Synaesthesia in art and music since 1900.* London: Thames & Hudson.

Büchel, C., Price, C. J., & Friston, K. J. (1998). A multimodal language region in the ventral visual pathway. *Nature, 6690,* 274–277.

Bushara, K. O., Hanakawa, T., Immisch, I., Toma, K., Kansaku, K., & Hallett, M. (2003). Neural correlates of cross-modal binding. *Nature Neuroscience, 6,* 190–195.

Calkins, M. W. (1895). Synaesthesia. *American Journal of Psychology, 7,* 90–107.

Callejas, A., Acosta, A., & Lupianez, J. (2007). Green love is ugly: Emotions elicited by synesthetic grapheme–color perceptions. *Brain Research, 1127,* 99–107.

Carlson, V. R. (1958). Effect of lysergic acid diethylamide (LSD-25) on the absolute visual threshold. *Journal of Comparative Physiological Psychology*, *51*, 528–531.

Chabalier, E. (1864). De la pseudochromesthésie. *Journal de Médicine de Lyon*, *102*.

Chrea, C., Valentin, D., Sulmont-Rossé, C., Ly Mai, H., Hoang Nguyen, D., & Abdi, H. (2004). Culture and odor categorization: Agreement between cultures depends upon the odors. *Food Quality and Preference*, *15*, 669–679.

Classen, C. (2005). *The book of touch*. Oxford: Berg Publishers.

Clinton, W. (2004). *My life*. New York: Alfred Knopf.

Cohen Kadosh, R., & Henik, A. (2006a). A common representation for semantic and physical properties. *Experimental Psychology*, *53*, 87–94.

Cohen Kadosh, R., & Henik, A. (2006b). When a line is a number: Color yields magnitude information in a digit–color synaesthete. *Neuroscience*, *137*, 3–5.

Colby, C. L., & Goldberg, M. E. (1999). Space and attention in parietal cortex. *Annual Review of Neuroscience*, *22*, 319–349.

Colman, W. S. (1894). Further remarks on colour-hearing. *Lancet*, *143*, 22.

Corballis, M. C. (2002). From mouth to hand: Gesture, speech, and the evolution of right-handedness. *Behavioral and Brain Sciences*, *26*, 199–260.

Cornaz, C. A. (1848). *Des abnormalités congénitales de jeux et de leurs annexes*. Lausanne: G. Bridel.

Craig, A. D. (2002). How do you feel? Interoception: the sense of the physiological condition of the body. *Nature Reviews Neuroscience*, *3*, 655–666.

Critchley, M. (1977). Ecstatic and synesthetic experience during musical perception. In M. Critchley & R. A. Henson (Eds.), *Music and Brain: Studies in the Neurology of Music*. Springfield, IL: Charles C Thomas.

Cutler, A., McQueen, J., & Robinson, K. (1990). Elizabeth and John: Sound pattern's of men's and women's names. *Journal of Linguistics*, *26*, 471–482.

Cytowic, R. E. (1993). *The man who tasted shapes*. London: Abacus Books.

Cytowic, R. E. (2002). *Synesthesia: A union of the senses* (2nd edition). Cambridge, MA: MIT Press.

Cytowic, R. E., & Wood, F. B. (1982). Synaesthesia II: Psychophysical relations in the synaesthesia of geometrically shaped taste and colored hearing. *Brain and Cognition*, *1*, 36–49.

Dalton, P., Doolittle, N., Nagata, H., & Breslin, P. A. S. (2000). The merging of the senses: Integration of subthreshold taste and smell. *Nature Neuroscience*, *3*, 431–432.

158   THE FROG WHO CROAKED BLUE

Dann, K. T. (1998). *Bright colors falsely seen*. New Haven, CT: Yale University Press.

Davis, R. (1961). The fitness of names to drawings: A cross-cultural study in Tanganyika. *British Journal of Psychology*, *52*, 259–268.

Day, S. (2005). Some demographic and socio-cultural aspects of synesthesia. In L. C. Robertson & N. Sagiv (Eds.), *Synesthesia: Perspectives from cognitive neuroscience*. Oxford: Oxford University Press.

Dehaene, S., Bossini, S., & Giraux, P. (1993). The mental representation of parity and numerical magnitude. *Journal of Experimental Psychology: General*, *122*, 371–396.

Dehaene, S., Dehaene-Lambertz, G., & Cohen, L. (1998). Abstract representations of numbers in the animal and human brain. *Trends in Neurosciences*, *21*, 355–361.

Dehay, C., Bullier, J., & Kennedy, H. (1984). Transient projections from the fronto-parietal and temporal cortex to areas 17, 18, 19 in the kitten. *Experimental Brain Research*, *57*, 208–212.

Dixon, M. J., Smilek, D., Cudahy, C., & Merikle, P. M. (2000). Five plus two equals yellow. *Nature*, *406*, 365.

Dixon, M. J., Smilek, D., & Merikle, P. M. (2004). Not all synaesthetes are created equal: Projector vs. associator synaesthetes. *Cognitive, Affective and Behavioral Neuroscience*, *4*, 335–343.

Downey, J. E. (1911). A case of colored gustation. *American Journal of Psychology*, *22*, 528–539.

Driver, J. (1996). Enhancement of selective listening by illusory mislocation of speech sounds due to lip-reading. *Nature*, *381*, 66–68.

Dudycha, G. J., & Dudycha, M. M. (1935). A case of synesthesia: Visual pain and visual audition. *Journal of Abnormal Psychology*, *30*, 57–69.

Duffy, P. L. (2001). *Blue cats and chartreuse kittens: How synaesthetes color their world*. New York: Times Books.

Dunbar, R. I. M. (1992). Neocortex size as a constraint on group size in primates. *Journal of Human Evolution*, *20*, 469–493.

Eimas, P. D. (1975). Auditory and phonetic coding of the cues for speech: Discrimination of the [r–l] distinction by young infants. *Perception & Psychophysics*, *18*, 341–347.

Feynman, R. (1988). *What do you care what other people think?* London: Unwin Paperbacks.

Finger, S., & Wade, N. J. (2002). The neuroscience of Helmholtz and the theories of Johannes Müller: Part 2. Sensation and perception. *Journal of the History of the Neurosciences*, *11*, 234–254.

Frank, R. A., & Byram, J. (1988). Taste–smell interactions are tastant and odorant dependent. *Chemical Senses*, *13*, 445–455.

Gallace, A., & Spence, C. (2006). Multisensory synesthetic interactions in the speeded classification of visual size. *Perception
and Psychophysics*, *68*, 1191–1203.

Galton, F. (1880). Statistics on mental imagery. *Mind*, *5*, 301–318.

Galton, F. (1883/1907/1973). *Inquiries into human faculty and its
development*. New York: AMS Press.

Gazzola, V., Aziz-Zadeh, L., & Keysers, C. (2006). Empathy and
the somatotopic auditory mirror system in humans. *Current
Biology*, *16*, 1824-1829.

Gevers, W., Reynvoet, B., & Fias, W. (2003). The mental representation of ordinal sequences is spatially organized. *Cognition*, *87*,
B87–B95.

Giray, E. F., Altkin, W. M., Vaught, G. M., & Roodin, P. A. (1976).
The incidence of eidetic imagery as a function of age. *Child
Development*, *47*, 1207–1210.

Goethe, J. H. (1810/1982). *Theory of Colours*. Cambridge, MA:
MIT Press.

Gregory, R. L., & Wallace, J. G. (1963). Recovery from early
blindness: A case study. *Experimental Psychology Society
Monograph 2*. London.

Guest, S., Catmur, C., Lloyd, D., & Spence, C. (2002). Audiotactile
interactions in roughness perception. *Experimental Brain
Research*, *146*, 161–171.

Gurgin, F. H., Evans, L., Dunphy, N., Klostermann, S., &
Simmons, K. (2007). Rubber hands feel the touch of light.
Psychological Science, *18*, 152–157.

Haber, R. N. (1979). Twenty years of haunting eidetic imagery:
Where's the ghost? *Behavioral and Brain Sciences*, *2*, 583-629.

Hancock, P. (2006). Monozygotic twins' colour–number association: A case study. *Cortex*, *42*, 147–150.

Hartman, A. M., & Hollister, L. E. (1963). Effect of mescaline,
lysergic acid diethylamide and psilocybin on color perception.
Psychopharmacolgia, *4*, 441–451.

Hill, E. L., & Frith, U. (2003). Understanding autism: Insights
from mind and brain. *Philosophical Transactions of the Royal
Society of London B*, *358*, 281–289.

Hofmann, A. (1980). *LSD: My Problem Child*: New York: McGraw-
Hill.

Hollowood, T. A., Linforth, R. S. T., & Taylor, A. (2002). The effect
of viscosity on the perception of flavour. *Chemical Senses*, *27*,
583-591.

Howells, T. H. (1944). The experimental development of color-tone
synesthesia. *Journal of Experimental Psychology*, *34*, 87–103.

Hull, J. M. (1990). *Touching the rock: An experience of blindness*.
New York: Vantage.

Huxley, A. (1954). *The doors of perception and heaven and hell*. London: Harper & Brothers.

Innocenti, G., & Clarke, S. (1984). Bilateral transitory projection to visual areas from auditory cortex in kittens. *Brain Research, 14*, 143–148.

Ione, A., & Tyler, C. (2004). Synesthesia: Is F-sharp colored violet? *Journal of the History of Neurosciences, 13*, 58–65.

Jacobs, L., Karpik, A., Bozian, D., & Gothgen, S. (1981). Auditory–visual synesthesia: Sound-induced photisms. *Archives of Neurology, 38*, 211–216.

James, W. (1890/1950). *The principles of psychology*. New York: Dover Publications.

Jespersen, O. (1933). Symbolic value of the vowel 'i'. *Linguistica: Selected papers of O. Jespersen in English, French and German*. Copenhagen, Denmark: Levin and Munksgaard.

Jewanski, J., & Ward, J. (in preparation). The colourful albino: Georg Sachs and the first medical account of synesthesia.

Kaiser, H. (1872). Association der worte mit farben. *Archiv für Augenheilkunde, XI*, 96.

Keeley, B. L. (2002). Making sense of the senses: Individuating modalities in humans and other animals. *Journal of Philosophy, 99*, 5–28.

Kennett, S., Taylor-Clarke, M., & Haggard, P. (2001). Noninformative vision improves the spatial resolution of touch in humans. *Current Biology, 11*, 1188–1191.

Kensinger, K. (1995). *How real people ought to live: The Cashinahua of Eastern Peru*. Prospect Heights, IL: Waveland Press.

Keverne, E. B., Martensz, N. D., & Tuite, B. (1989). Beta-endorphin concentrations in cerebrospinal fluid of monkeys are influenced by grooming relationships. *Psychoneuroendocrinology, 14*, 155–161.

Keysers, C., Wicker, B., Gazzola, V., Anton, J. L., Fogassi, L., & Gallese, V. (2004). A touching sight: SII/PV activation during the observation and experience of touch. *Neuron, 42*, 335–346.

Krill, A. E., Alpert, H. J., & Ostfeld, A. M. (1963). Effects of a hallucinogenic agent in totally blind subjects. *Archives of Othalmology, 69*, 180–185.

Krohn, W. O. (1892). Pseudo-chromesthesia, or the association of colors with words, letters and sounds. *American Journal of Psychology, 5*, 20–41.

Kupers, R., Fumal, A., de Noordhout, A. M., Gjedde, A., Schoenen, J., & Ptito, M. (2006). Transcranial magnetic stimulation of the visual cortex induces somatotopically organized qualia in blind subjects. *Proceedings of the National Academy of Science, USA, 103*, 13256–13260.

Leary, T. (1968). *High Priest*. Cleveland, OH: World Publishing Company.

Lee, M. A., & Shlain, B. (1985). *Acid dreams: The complete social history of LSD – the CIA, the sixties and beyond*. New York: Grove Press.

Lewkowicz, D., & Turkewitz, G. (1980). Cross-modal equivalence in infancy: Auditory–visual intensity matching. *Developmental Psychology*, *16*, 597–607.

Lindstrom, M. (2005). *Brand sense: How to build powerful brands through touch, taste, smell, sight and sound*. London: Kogan Page.

Luria, A. (1968). *The mind of a mnemonist*. New York: Basic Books.

Lussana, F. (1873). *Fisiolgia dei colori*. Padova, Italy.

Marks, L. E. (1975). On coloured-hearing synaesthesia: Cross-modal translations of sensory dimensions. *Psychological Bulletin*, *82*, 303–331.

Marks, L. E. (1982a). Bright sneezes and dark coughs, loud sunlight and soft moonlight. *Journal of Experimental Psychology: Human Perception and Performance*, *8*, 177–193.

Marks, L. E. (1982b). Synesthetic perception and poetic metaphor. *Journal of Experimental Psychology: Human Perception and Performance*, *8*, 15–23.

Marks, L. (1987). On cross-modal similarity: Auditory–visual interactions in speeded discrimination. *Journal of Experimental Psycholoy: Human Perception and Performance*, *13*, 384-394.

Mattingley, J. B., Payne, J., & Rich, A. N. (2006). Attentional load attenuates synaesthetic priming effects in grapheme–colour synaesthesia. *Cortex*, *42*, 213–221.

Maurer, D. (1997). Neonatal synaesthesia: Implications for the processing of speech and faces. In S. Baron-Cohen & J. E. Harrison (Eds.), *Synaesthesia: Classic and contemporary readings*. Oxford: Blackwell.

Maurer, D., & Maurer, C. (1988). *The world of the newborn*. New York: Basic Books.

Maurer, D., & Mondloch, C. J. (2006). The infant as synesthete? *Attention and Performance*, *XXI*, 449–471.

Maurer, D., Pathman, T., & Mondloch, C. J. (2006). The shape of boubas: Sound–shape correspondences in toddlers and adults. *Developmental Science*, *9*, 316–322.

McDonell, P. (1990). Kandinsky: Early theories on synaesthesia. *Art Criticism*, *6*, 28–42.

McGurk, H., & MacDonald, J. (1976). Hearing lips and seeing voices. *Nature*, *264*, 746–748.

Meltzoff, A. N., & Borton, R. W. (1979). Intermodal matching by human neonates. *Nature*, *282*, 403–404.

Merabet, L. B., Maguire, D., Warde, A., Alterescu, K., Stickgold, R., & Pascual-Leone, A. (2004). Visual hallucinations during prolonged blindfolding in sighted subjects. *Journal of Neuro-opthalmology*, *24*, 109–113.

Mills, C. B., Innis, J., Westendorf, T., Owsianiecki, L., & McDonald, A. (2006). Influence of a synesthete's photisms on name recall. *Cortex*, *42*, 155–163.

Mills, C. B., Viguers, M. L., Edelson, S. K., Thomas, A. T., Simon-Dack, S. L., & Innis, J. A. (2002). The color of two alphabets for a multilingual synesthete. *Perception*, *31*, 1371–1394.

Mitchell, S. W. (1866). The case of George Dedlow. *Atlantic Monthly*.

Mollon, J. D. (1991). Uses and evolutionary origins of primate colour vision. In J. R. Cronly-Dillon & R. L. Gregory (Eds.), *Evolution of the eye and the visual system*. London: Macmillan Press.

Mondloch, C. J., & Maurer, D. (2004). Do small white balls squeak? Pitch–object correspondences in young children. *Cognitive, Affective and Behavioral Neuroscience*, *4*, 133–136.

Morgan, M. (1977). *Molyneux's question: Vision, touch and the philosophy of perception*. Cambridge: Cambridge University Press.

Morgan, M. (2003). *The space between our ears: How the brain represents visual space*. Oxford: Oxford University Press.

Morrot, G., Brochet, F., & Dubourdieu, D. (2001). The color of odors. *Brain and Language*, *79*, 309–320.

Murray, M. M., Michel, C. M., Grave de Peralta, R., Ortigue, S., Brunet, D., Gonzalez Andino, S., & Schnider, A. (2004). Rapid discrimination of visual and multisensory memories revealed by electrical neuroimaging. *NeuroImage*, *21*, 125–135.

Nabokov, V. (1967). *Speak, memory: An autobiography revisited*. New York: Vintage Books.

Nettle, D., & Clegg, H. (2006). Schizotypy, creativity and mating success in humans. *Proceedings of the Royal Society of London B*, *273*, 611–615.

Neville, H. J. (1995). Developmental specificity in neurocognitive development in humans. In M. Gazzaniga (Ed.), *The Cognitive Neurosciences*. Cambridge, MA: MIT Press.

Nunn, J. A., Gregory, L. J., Brammer, M., Williams, S. C. R., Parslow, D. M., Morgan, M. J., Morris, R. G., Bullmore, E. T., Baron-Cohen, S., & Gray, J. A. (2002). Functional magnetic resonance imaging of synesthesia: Activation of V4/V8 by spoken words. *Nature Neuroscience*, *5*, 371–375.

Oberman, L. M., Hubbard, E. M., McCleery, J. P., Altschuler, E. L., Ramachandran, V. S., & Pineda, J. A. (2005). EEG evidence for mirror neuron dysfunction in autism spectrum disorders. *Cognitive Brain Research*, *24*, 190–198.

Odgaard, E. C., Arieh, Y., & Marks, L. E. (2004). Brighter noise: Sensory enhancement of perceived loudness by concurrent visual stimulation. *Cognitive, Affective and Behavioral Neuroscience*, *4*, 127–132.

O'Sullivan, S. D. (2006). Synaesthesia: What's in a word? *Meeting of UK Synaesthesia Association*. London, 22–23 April.

Peacock, K. (1988). Instruments to perform color-music: Two centuries of technological exploration. *Leonardo*, *21*, 397–406.

Perroud, M. (1863). De l'hyperchromatopsie. *Memoires et Comptes Rendus de la Societé Médicale de Lyon.*

Piazza, M., Pinel, P., & Dehaene, S. (2006). Objective correlates of an unusual subjective experience: A single-case study of number-form synaesthesia. *Cognitive Neuropsychology*, *23*, 1162–1173.

Ramachandran, V. S., & Hirstein, W. (1998). The perception of phantom limbs. *Brain*, *121*, 1603–1630.

Ramachandran, V. S., & Hubbard, E. M. (2001a). Psychophysical investigations into the neural basis of synaesthesia. *Proceedings of the Royal Society of London B*, *268*, 979–983.

Ramachandran, V. S., & Hubbard, E. M. (2001b). Synaesthesia – A window into perception, thought and language. *Journal of Consciousness Studies*, *8*, 3–34.

Ramachandran, V. S., & Hubbard, E. M. (2003). Hearing colors, tasting shapes. *Scientific American*, April, 52–59.

Ramachandran, V. S., & Rogers-Ramachandran, D. (1996). Synaesthesia in phantom limbs induced with mirrors. *Proceedings of the Royal Society of London B*, *263*, 377–386.

Ramachandran, V. S., Rogers-Ramachandran, D., & Cobb, S. (1995). Touching the phantom limb. *Nature*, *377*, 489–490.

Rao, A. L., Nobre, A. C., Alexander, I., & Cowey, A. (2007). Auditory evoked visual awareness following sudden ocular blindness: an EEG and TMS investigation. *Experimental Brain Research*, *176*, 288–298.

Regier, T., Kay, P., & Khetarpal, N. (2007). Color naming reflects optimal partitions of color space. *Proceedings of the National Academy of Science, USA*, *104*, 1436–1441.

Rich, A. N., Bradshaw, J. L., & Mattingley, J. B. (2005). A systematic, large-scale study of synaesthesia: Implications for the role of early experience in lexical–colour associations. *Cognition*, *98*, 53–84.

Rich, A. N., & Mattingley, J. B. (2003). The effects of stimulus competition and voluntary attention on colour–graphemic synaesthesia. *NeuroReport*, *14*, 1793–1798.

Riggs, L. A., & Karwoski, T. (1934). Synaesthesia. *British Journal of Psychology, 25*, 29–41.

Rizzolatti, G., & Arbib, M. A. (1998). Language within our grasp. *Trends in Neuroscience, 21*, 188–194.

Rizzolatti, G., Fogassi, L., & Gallese, V. (2001). Neuropsychological mechanisms underlying the understanding and execution of action. *Nature Reviews Neuroscience, 2*, 661–670.

Sachs, G. T. L. (1812). *Historiae naturalis duorum leucaetiopum: Auctoris ipsius et sororis ei us*. Solisbaci, Germany: Sumptibus Bibliopolii Seideliani.

Sacks, O. (1985). *The man who mistook his wife for a hat*. London: Picador.

Sacks, O. (1995). *An anthropologist on mars*. London: Picador.

Sadato, N., Pascual-Leone, A., Grafman, J., Ibanez, V., Deiber, M.-P., Dold, G., & Hallett, M. (1996). Activation of primary visual cortex by Braille reading in blind subjects. *Nature, 380*, 526–528.

Sagiv, N., Simner, J., Collins, J., Butterworth, B., & Ward, J. (2006). What is the relationship between synaesthesia and visuo-spatial number forms? *Cognition, 101*, 114–128.

Sapir, E. (1929). A study in phonetic symbolism. *Journal of Experimental Psychology, 12*, 239–255.

Schlegel, J. H. G. (1824). *Ein beitrag zur nahern kenntnis der albinos*. Meiningen, Germany: Keyssner.

Shams, L., Kamitani, Y., & Shimojo, S. (2000). Illusions: What you see is what you hear. *Nature, 408*, 788.

Shams, L., Kamitani, Y., Thompson, S., & Shimojo, S. (2001). Sound alters visual evoked potentials in humans. *NeuroReport, 12*, 3849–3852.

Shanon, B. (1982). Colour associates to semantic linear orders. *Psychological Research, 44*, 75–83.

Simner, J., & Holenstein, E. (2007). Ordinal linguistic personification as a variant of synesthesia. *Journal of Cognitive Neuroscience, 19*, 694–703.

Simner, J., Lanz, M., Jansari, A., Noonan, K., Glover, L., Oakley, D. A., & Ward, J. (2005). Non-random associations of graphemes to colours in synaesthetic and normal populations. *Cognitive Neuropsychology, 22*, 1069–1085.

Simner, J., Mulvenna, C., Sagiv, N., Tsakanikos, E., Witherby, S. A., Fraser, C., Scott, K., & Ward, J. (2006). Synaesthesia: The prevalence of atypical cross-modal experiences. *Perception, 35*, 1024–1033.

Simons, D. J., & Chabris, C. F. (1999). Gorillas in our midst: Sustained inattentional blindness for dynamic events. *Perception, 28*, 1059–1074.

Singer, T., Seymour, B., O'Doherty, J., Kaube, H., Dolan, R. J., &

Frith, C. D. (2004). Empathy for pain involves the affective but not the sensory components of pain. *Science*, *303*, 1157–1162.

Smilek, D., Callejas, A., Merikle, P., & Dixon, M. (2006). Ovals of time: Space–time synesthesia. *Consciousness and Cognition*, *16*, 507–519.

Smilek, D., Dixon, M. J., Cudahy, C., & Merikle, P. M. (2002a). Synaesthetic color experiences influence memory. *Psychological Science*, *13*, 548–552.

Smilek, D., Dixon, M. J., & Merikle, P. M. (2005). Synaesthesia: Discordant male monozygotic twins. *Neurocase*, *11*, 363–370.

Smilek, D., Malcolmson, K A., Carriere, J. S., Eller, M., Kwan, D., & Reynolds, M. (2007). When '3' is a jerk and '0' is a king: Personifying inanimate objects in synesthesia. *Journal of Cognitive Neuroscience*, *19*, 981–992.

Smilek, D., Moffatt, B. A., Pasternak, J., White, B. N., Dixon, M. J., & Merikle, P. M. (2002b). Synaesthesia: A case study of discordant monozygotic twins. *Neurocase*, *8*, 338–342.

Spector, F., & Maurer, D. (in press). The color of O's: Naturally-biased associations between shape and color. *Perception*.

Steen, C. J. (2001). Visions shared: A firsthand look into synesthesia and art. *Leonardo*, *34*, 203–208.

Stein, B. E., Honeycutt, W. S., & Meredith, M. A. (1988). Neurons and behavior: The same rules of multisensory integration apply. *Brain Research*, *448*, 355–358.

Stein, B. E., London, N., Wilkinson, L. K., & Price, D. D. (1996). Enhancement of perceived visual intensity by auditory stimuli: A psychophysical analysis. *Journal of Cognitive Neuroscience*, *8*, 497–506.

Stein, B. E., & Meredith, M. A. (1993). *The Merging of the Senses*. Cambridge, MA: MIT Press.

Steven, M. S., & Blakemore, C. (2004). Visual synaesthesia in the blind. *Perception*, *33*, 855–868.

Stevens (1892). Colors of letters. *Popular Science Monthly*, March.

Stevenson, R. J., Boakes, R. A., & Wilson, J. P. (2000). Counter conditioning following human odor–taste and color–taste learning. *Learning and Motivation*, *31*, 114–127.

Stevenson, R. J., Miller, L. A., & Thayer, Z. C. (in press). Impairments in the perception of odor-induced tastes and their relationship to impairments in taste perception. *Journal of Experimental Psychology: Human Perception and Performance*.

Stevenson, R. J., & Tomiczek, C. (2007). Olfactory-induced synesthesias: A review and model. *Psychological Bulletin*, *133*, 294–309.

Streri, A. (1987). Tactile discrimination of shape and inter-modal transfer in 2- to 3-month old infants. *British Journal of Developmental Psychology*, *5*, 213–220.

Stroop, J. R. (1935). Studies of interference in serial verbal reactions. *Journal of Experimental Psychology: General, 106*, 404–426.

Sumby, W. H., & Pollack, I. (1954). Visual contribution to speech intelligibilty in noise. *Journal of the Acoustical Society of America, 26*, 212–215.

Tammet, D. (2006). *Born on a blue day*. London: Hodder & Stoughton.

Verhagen, J. V., & Engelen, L. (2006). The neurocognitive bases of human multimodal food perception: sensory integration. *Neuroscience and Biobehavioral Review, 30*, 613–650.

Vroomen, J., & de Gelder, B. (2000). Sound enhances visual perception: Cross-modal effects of auditory organisation on vision. *Journal of Experimental Psychology: Human Perception and Performance, 26*, 1583–1590.

Wagner, S., Winner, E., Cicchetti, D., & Gardner, H. (1981). 'Metaphorical' mapping in human infants. *Child Development, 52*, 728–731.

Ward, J. (2004). Emotionally mediated synaesthesia. *Cognitive Neuropsychology, 71*, 761–772.

Ward, J., Collins, J., Sarri, M., Sagiv, N., & Butterworth, B. (submitted). Synaesthesia, number forms and difficulties in arithmetic.

Ward, J., Huckstep, B., & Tsakanikos, E. (2006a). Sound–colour synaesthesia: To what extent does it use cross-modal mechanisms common to us all? *Cortex, 42*, 264–280.

Ward, J., Moore, S., Thompson-Lake, D., Salih, S., & Beck, B. (in press a). The aesthetics of visual music: Why audio-visual synaesthetic perceptions are appealing. *Perception*.

Ward, J., & Sagiv, N. (2007). Synaesthesia for finger counting and dice patterns: A case of higher synaesthesia? *NeuroCase, 13*, 86–93.

Ward, J., Li, R., Salih, S., & Sagiv, N. (2007). Varieties of grapheme–colour synaesthesia: A new theory of phenomenological and behavioural differences. *Consciousness and Cognition 16*, 913–931.

Ward, J., & Simner, J. (2003). Lexical-gustatory synaesthesia: Linguistic and conceptual factors. *Cognition, 89*, 237–261.

Ward, J., Simner, J., & Auyeung, V. (2005). A comparison of lexical–gustatory and grapheme–colour synaesthesia. *Cognitive Neuropsychology, 22*, 28–41.

Ward, J., Thompson-Lake, D., Ely, R., & Kaminski, F. (in press b). Synaesthesia, creativity and art: What is the link? *British Journal of Psychology*.

Ward, J., Tsakanikos, E., & Bray, A. (2006b). Synaesthesia for reading and playing musical notes. *Neurocase, 12*, 27–34.

Wartmann, E. F. (1849). *Deuxieme mémorie sur le daltonisme.* Geneva: Fick.

Wasson, R. G., Hofmann, A., & Ruck, C. A. P. (1978). *The road to Eleusis: Unveiling the secret of the mysteries.* New York: Harcourt Brace Jovanovich.

Weeks, R., Horwitz, B., Aziz-Sultan, A., Tian, B., Wessinger, C. M., Cohen, L., Hallett, M., & Rauschecker, J. P. (2000). A positron emission tomographic study of auditory localization in the congenitally blind. *Journal of Neuroscience, 20,* 2664–2672.

Westbury, C. (2005). Implicit sound symbolism in lexical access: Evidence from an interference task. *Brain and Language, 93,* 10–19.

Wheeler, R. H., & Cutsforth, T. D. (1921a). The number forms of a blind subject. *American Journal of Psychology, 32,* 21–25.

Wheeler, R. H., & Cutsforth, T. D. (1921b). The role of synaesthesia in learning. *Journal of Experimental Psychology, 4,* 448–468.

Wicker, B., Keysers, C., Plailly, J., Royet, J. P., Gallese, V., & Rizzolatti, G. (2003). Both of us disgusted in my insula: The common neural basis of seeing and feeling disgust. *Neuron, 40,* 655–664.

Wilding, J., & Valentine, E. (1997). *Superior memory.* Hove, UK: Psychology Press.

Witthoft, N., & Winawer, J. (2006). Synesthetic colors determined by having colored refrigerator magnets in childhood. *Cortex, 42,* 175–183.

Wolff, P., Matsumiya, Y., Abrohms, I. F., van Velzer, C., & Lambroso, C. T. (1974). The effect of white noise on the somatosensory evoked responses in sleeping newborn infants. *Electroencephalography and Clinical Neurophysiology, 37,* 269–274.

Wollen, K. A., & Ruggiero, F. T. (1983). Coloured-letter synaesthesia. *Journal of Mental Imagery, 7,* 83–86.

Yaro, C., & Ward, J. (2007). Searching for Shereshevskii: What is superior about the memory of synaesthetes? *Quarterly Journal of Experimental Psychology, 60,* 682–696.

Yendrikhovskij, S. N. (2001). Computing color categories from statistics of natural images. *Journal of Imaging Science and Technology, 45,* 409–417.

Yeomans, M. R., Mobini, S., Elliman, T. D., Walker, H. C., & Stevenson, R. J. (2006). Hedonic and sensory characteristics of odors conditioned by pairing with tastants in humans. *Journal of Experimental Psychology: Animal Behavior Processes, 32,* 215–228.

Zampini, M., Guest, S., & Spence, C. (2003). The role of auditory cues in modulating the perception of electric toothbrushes. *Journal of Dental Research*, *82*, 929–932.

Zampini, M., & Spence, C. (2004). The role of auditory cues in modulating the perceived crispness and staleness of potato chips. *Journal of Sensory Science*, *19*, 347–363.

Zampini, M., & Spence, C. (2005). Modifying the multisensory perception of a carbonated beverage using auditory cues. *Food Quality and Preference*, *16*, 632–641.

Zeki, S. (1993). *A vision of the brain*. Oxford: Blackwell.

Zellner, D. A., Bartoli, A. M., & Eckard, R. (1991). Influence of color on odor identification and liking ratings. *American Journal of Psychology*, *104*, 547–561.

Zellner, D. A., & Kautz, M. A. (1990). Color affects perceived odour intensity. *Journal of Experimental Psychology*, *16*, 391–397.

Zigler, M. J. (1930). Tone shapes: A novel type of synaesthesia. *Journal of General Psychology*, *3*, 277–286.

Index

achromatopsia 24–5
acquired synesthesia 62,
68–72, 93, 102–3
adjacency 63–4
after-images 12–13
albinos 1, 2, 112
alphabet books 7, 63
Alternate Uses Test 130, 131
animation 129–30
Aristotle 31–3, 70, 113
art 25, 63, 118, 119, 126–30,
138
associators 98–100
attention 83, 84–5
auras 101–2
autism 111–13, 124

babies 19, 36–40; *see also*
infants
Bach-y-Rita, Paul 22–3
balance 33, 35, 51
Barnum, Phineas 1
Baron-Cohen, Simon 27, 29,
42
behaviorism 15–16
Berlin, Brent 79, 81
Bleuler, Eugene 14
blind spot 102–3
blindfolding 21, 28, 62, 69
blindness 9, 16–26, 29, 32, 62;
inattentional 83;
intersensory pathways 40,

69–70; Molyneux's question
16–17, 18, 39; partial
102–3
Blumenthal, Heston 54–5
Bradford, Sydney 18–19
Braille 17, 20, 68
brain 12–13, 15, 57–8, 62;
achromatopsia 24–5;
acquired synesthesia 69;
adjacency principle 63–4;
babies 37–8, 39; blindness
20, 40, 69–70; creativity 127;
hallucinogenic drug use 21,
72; mirror system 123–4,
125, 133–4; multisensory
perception 46, 47–8, 52, 60,
86–7; numbers 104; phantom
limbs 92–3; sensory
information 35; spatial maps
89–90, 91, 96–7, 109, 110,
116; taste 45, 66; touch
121–2, 123–4; V4 region
23–4, 28, 29–30, 49, 63;
visual stimulation 23, 28, 29,
47–8, 121–2
brain imaging 20, 28, 29, 46,
121–2

Calkins, Mary 14–15
cerebral achromatopsia 24–5
Chabris, Christopher 83
Cheselden, William 18

children 80, 101, 103, 133; *see also* infants
Chinese language 67
Clinton, Bill 120
cola drinks 56–7
color 1–2, 4–5, 9–10, 60–1, 65, 73–4; achromatopsia 24–5; auras 101–2; Baron-Cohen's cases 27; blind people's experience of 17–18, 32; brain regions 23–4, 28, 29–30, 49, 57–8, 62, 63, 66; days of the week 81; famous synesthetes 11–12; first letter of words 43; food 54, 56–7; Goethe's theory of 12–13; hallucinogenic drug use 21, 72; impact on odor intensity 57; memory 13–14, 136, 137; music 74–8; names 5–6; numbers 64–5, 78, 106; ordering 78–81; spatial location 90, 98–100; Stroop tasks 83–6; testing for synesthesia 10–11; twins 6–7
color blindness 13, 24, 40
communication 118
Cornaz, Edward 13
creativity 117, 126–31, 138
cultural differences 41, 67–8
Curtis, Edgar xiii
Cutsforth, Thomas 17, 23
Cytowic, Richard 26–7, 29, 124, 128

Dalton, Pamela 50
Darwin, Charles 14
dates 106–8
Day, Sean 9
days of the week 2, 11, 42, 81, 106–8
Dedlow, George 91–2
Dehaene, Stanislas 104
Diderot, Denis 19
Dixon, Mike 98–9, 106
DNA samples 8

doctrine of specific nerve energies 49
double flash illusion 47
drugs 9, 21–2, 26, 29, 35, 62, 70–2, 75
Dudycha, G. J. 34
Dudycha, M. M. 34
Duffy, Pat 59, 67, 98
Dunbar, Robin 10

emotions 82, 120; auras 102; mirror systems 123, 124
empathy 122, 123, 138
endorphins 121
environmental factors 16, 67
evolution 125, 126, 128–9, 137, 138

families 6, 7, 8–9
Feynman, Richard 11, 111
flavor 26, 42–5, 52–7, 65–6; *see also* taste
Fletcher, Pat 22, 93
food 40–1, 52–7
Freud, Sigmund 15

Galton, Francis 14, 98
gender 66
genetics 7, 8–9, 125, 126
Gershwin, George 128
Goethe, Johann Wolfgang von 12

habituation 38
hallucinations 21, 23
hallucinogenic drugs 9, 21–2, 26, 29, 35, 62, 70–2, 75
hand gestures 133, 134
handedness 105, 112
hearing 32, 33; awareness of 35; babies' response to sound 37–9; blind people 19, 20, 23; colored 28, 30; impact on flavor intensity 57; multisensory perception 46–51; *see also* sounds

Hockney, David 128
Hoffmann, Albert 21, 71–2
Hubbard, Ed 126–7, 131, 132
Hull, John 19–20

illusions 30, 46, 50, 51–2;
    double flash illusion 47;
    McGurk illusion 48; rubber
    hand illusion 94–5
imagery 103–4, 113, 116; *see
    also* mental images
inattentional blindness 83
infants 36–40, 76, 77; *see also*
    children
interoception 33, 34, 35

James, William 15, 36

Kaiser, Dr 13
Kandinsky, Wassily 127–8
Kay, Paul 79, 81
Keverne, Barry 121
Kipling, Rudyard 76
Köhler, Wolfgang 132

language: color names 79;
    cultural factors 67–8;
    evolution 131–5, 137–8;
    infants' language ability
    39–40; learning a new 111,
    118; mirror systems 124;
    pitch 77; taste/word
    associations 44, 66; *see also*
    letters; speech; words
Lehmann, Karl 14
letters 2, 7, 42, 60–1, 63, 65;
    associators 99; Baron-
    Cohen's cases 27; brain
    regions 66; color ordering 80;
    cultural factors 67–8; first
    letter of words 43; musical
    notation 68; Nabokov 11;
    projectors 98–9, 100; *see also*
    language; words
Lewkowicz, David 38
lip-reading 48, 50–1

loci, method of 113, 115
Locke, John 16, 17, 18, 32,
    39
LSD 9, 21–2, 26, 29, 35, 62,
    70–2

Mackay, Jane 128
maps 89–91, 96–7, 98, 100–1,
    108–10, 115, 116
Marks, Larry 75, 76
maths 105–6, 118
Mattingley, Jason 85
Maurer, Charles 37
Maurer, Daphne 37, 38, 39, 42,
    76
McGurk illusion 48
Meijer, Peter 22
memory 13–14, 27, 117–18,
    135–8; dates 107, 108;
    numbers 106; Shereshevskii
    114–16; Tammet 110–11,
    112–14
mental images 14, 103–4; *see
    also* imagery
Messiaen, Olivier 128
method of loci 113, 115
Mills, Carol 67
mind's eye 14, 64, 98, 99, 100,
    101, 103
mirror systems 123–5, 133–4
mirror touch 119–20, 121–5,
    138
Molyneux's question 16–17, 18,
    39
Mondloch, Cathy 76
months 97–8, 106–8
Moore, Samantha 129
Müller, Johannes 49
multisensory perception 40–1,
    45, 46–52, 69, 72–3, 125–6;
    babies 37–8; coordinate
    transformations 97; food
    52–7; language evolution
    135; mirror touch 121, 123,
    124; synesthesia similarity to
    59, 60–2, 74, 86–7

music 2, 3, 128, 131; notation
    68; spatial location 101;
    visualized 69, 72, 74–8, 129,
    138

Nabokov, Vladimir 11
names 2, 3, 5–6, 135
nerve cells 13–14, 28, 37, 48–9,
    123
nerve energies, doctrine of
    specific 49
neurons 48–9, 50
Newton, Isaac 12, 75
novelty 130, 131
number forms 4, 98, 105–6
numbers 2, 4, 42, 63, 64–5, 78;
    maths 118; Shereshevskii
    114–15; spatial arrangement
    of 4, 97, 98, 104–6; Tammet
    110–11, 112–13
Nunn, Julia 28

orgasms 9

pain 15, 33, 34; color of 3;
    mirror system 124, 125
parietal lobes 97, 109
Pascual-Leone, Alvaro 21
perception 36, 45, 72–3, 83;
    see also multisensory
    perception
phantom limbs 87, 91–3
phonemes 40
pi 110–11
pitch 19, 60, 75–7, 78, 81, 87,
    134
Plato 70
Poe, Edgar Allan 76
poetry 76, 126–7
prevalence 10–11, 122, 125
projectors 98–100
proprioception 33–4, 35, 61,
    103; phantom limbs 93;
    rubber hand illusion 94;
    space 96, 97

Ramachandran, V. S. xi, 63,
    126–7, 131, 132
Remote Associates Test
    130–1
retina 13, 32, 33, 95, 96, 103
rubber hand illusion 94–5

Sachs, George 1–2, 6, 8, 12, 13,
    23, 30, 68
Sacks, Oliver 25, 34, 82
Schlegel, Julius 1, 13
science 12, 15, 16, 29, 126,
    138
sensation 36, 37, 90
senses 31–6; babies 36–40;
    blind people 19, 20, 23; food
    52–7; integration of 21;
    Shereshevskii 115; space 95,
    97; see also multisensory
    perception
sensory receptors 32, 33, 34, 36,
    48
sensory substitution devices
    22–3, 93
sequences 110–11, 113,
    115–16, 136
shape 26, 27, 80
Shelley, Percy 76
Shereshevskii, Solomon
    114–16, 135–6
sign language 133, 134
Simner, Julia xii, 10, 44
Simons, Daniel 83
Skinner, B. F. 15, 16
smell 10, 31–2, 33; colored 101;
    food 40–1; lack of awareness
    of 35; mirror system 124;
    multisensory perception 50,
    57, 60
social behavior 120–1
sounds 2, 3, 32, 74–8; babies'
    response to 37–9; blind
    people's experience of 19–20,
    22; food names 44; languages
    39–40; multisensory
    perception 46–51, 60, 125;

pitch 19, 60, 75–7, 78, 81, 87, 134; Shereshevskii 115; space 97, 101; *see also* hearing

space 64, 87, 89–116; memory 110–16; numbers 104–6; pitch relationship to spatial positioning 77; projector-associator distinction 98–100; rubber hand illusion 94–5; time 106–8; types of 95–103

speech: language evolution 134; lip-reading 48, 50–1; multisensory perception 50–1, 61; phonemes 40; spatial location 101; *see also* language

Stanton, Philippa 128

Steen, Carol 3, 8, 9–10

Stevenson, Richard 41

Stewart-Jones, Elizabeth 27

Stoll, Werner 71

Stroop test 83–4

synesthesia xi–xii, 3–12; acquired 62, 68–72, 93, 102–3; adjacency principle 63–4; advantages of 125–6, 135, 138; babies 37, 38; blindness 16–26, 69–70; choice of colors 73–4; color ordering 79, 80; consequences of 61, 62–3, 119, 138–9; creativity 126–31, 138; famous synesthetes 11–12; hallucinogenic drugs 21–2; language evolution 131–5, 137–8; memory 110–16, 117–18, 135–8; model of 61–3, 67, 86–7; modern research on 26–30; multisensory perception similarity to 59, 60–2, 74, 86–7; numbers 105–6; phantom limbs 93; rise and fall of 12–16; rubber hand

illusion 95; Sachs 2; senses 34–5, 42; space 64, 89–90, 97–103, 108–10, 116; strengths and weakness of 117–18; taste 42–5, 55–6, 65–6; time 106–8; touch 119–25; turning off 81–6; vivid visual imagery 103–4

Tammet, Daniel 110–14, 118, 135–6, 138

taste 26–7, 32, 33, 40–1; awareness of 35; mirror system 124; multisensory perception 50, 52–7, 60; Shereshevskii 115; words associated with 7, 42–5, 55–6, 65–6

temperature 32, 33, 34, 109

time 106–8, 131

touch 32, 33, 69, 119–25; awareness of 35; babies 38, 39; blind people 19, 20, 23, 103; darkness impact on 53–4; impact on flavor intensity 57; multisensory illusions 51; phantom limbs 93; rubber hand illusion 94–5; sensory substitution devices 22–3; Shereshevskii 115; space 97

Turkewitz, Gerald 38

twins 6–7, 8–9

V4 region 23–4, 28, 29–30, 49, 63

Valentine, Elizabeth 137

ventriloquism 50, 95

vestibular sense (balance) 33, 35, 51

vision 9, 13, 20, 32, 33; achromatopsia 25; awareness of 35, 86; babies' response to stimulation 38–9; brain regions 23–4; hallucinogenic drug use 72; multisensory

perception 46–51, 60–1, 125;
retinal receptors 32, 33;
rubber hand illusion 94–5;
sensory substitution devices
22; Shereshevskii 115; space
97; touch 103; *see also*
blindness

Wannerton, James 7, 42–5, 53,
55–6, 65, 129
Watson, Michael 26–7, 54–5
Whistler, James McNeill 127

Wilding, John 137
wine 57
Wittgenstein, Ludwig 11–12
words 2, 3, 5; Baron-Cohen's
cases 27; brain regions 28;
language evolution 131–5;
Stroop test 83–4; taste
association with 7, 42–5,
55–6, 65–6; *see also*
language; letters

Zeki, Semir 23–4

Further information on the web

A website accompanies this book at:
www.thefrogwhocroakedblue. com

The author's website is: www.syn.sussex.ac.uk

UK Synaesthesia Association: www.uksynaesthesia.com

American Synesthesia Association: www.synesthesia.info

Sean Day's email discussion list ('SynList'): home. comcast.net/
~sean.day/Synesthesia.htm